GUIDANCE

&
OTHER SMALL-GROUP
COUNSELING TOPICS
FOR
MIDDLE SCHOOL STUDENTS

WRITTEN BY
Becky Kirby

ILLUSTRATED BY
Jeffrey Zwartjes

ABOUT THE AUTHOR

Becky Fesemyer Kirby has been an educator for 33 years and a middle school counselor for the past 15 years. Becky works with seventh- and eighth-grade students at Brown Middle School in Ravenna, Ohio.

Becky received an undergraduate degree from Kent State University. She received a master's degree in school counseling from the same university.

Becky lives in Ravenna with her husband David. Their three children, Kristine, Greg, and Jeff, are all graduates of Ohio State University.

Grab Bag Guidance

10-DIGIT ISBN: 1-57543-133-5   13-DIGIT ISBN: 978-1-57543-133-8

REPRINTED 2007
COPYRIGHT © 2005 MAR*CO PRODUCTS, INC.
Published by mar*co products, inc.
1443 Old York Road
Warminster, PA 18974
1-800-448-2197
www.marcoproducts.com

PERMISSION TO REPRODUCE: The purchaser may reproduce the activity sheets, free and without special permission, for participant use for a particular group or class. Reproduction of these materials for an entire school system is forbidden.

All rights reserved. Except as provided above, no part of this book may be reproduced or transmitted in whole or in part in any form or by any means, electronic or mechanical, including photocopying, recording, or by any information storage or retrieval system without permission in writing by the publisher.

PRINTED IN THE U.S.A.

CONTENTS

INTRODUCTION 7
    USING THE GROUP OPENING AND GROUP RULES IN GROUP SESSIONS 8
    GROUP OPENING 9
    GROUP RULES 10

ENERGIZERS & EXTRAS 11
    USING THE ENERGIZERS IN GROUP SESSIONS 12
    ENERGIZER 1: INTRODUCTION 13
    ENERGIZER 2: LISTENING GAME 14
    ENERGIZER 3: TELLING ABOUT YOURSELF 22
    ENERGIZER 4: FEELINGS CUBE 23
    ENERGIZER 5: SENTENCE STRIPS 24
    ENERGIZER 6: FEELING CARDS 25
    ENERGIZER 7: SNOWBALL FUN 30
    ENERGIZER 8: YARN BALL REVIEW 31
    ENERGIZER 9: TRUTH OR LIE? 31
    ENERGIZER 10: SOMETHING I LIKED 32
    ENERGIZER 11: STRENGTHS 32
    ENERGIZER 12: DECISION-MAKING 33
    ENERGIZER 13: LIKENESS LETTER 33
    ENERGIZER 14: A BROKEN HEART 34
    ENERGIZER 15: ESCALATOR 34
    ENERGIZER 16: A TO Z STORY 35
    ENERGIZER 17: PEOPLE/POSSESSIONS 35
    ENERGIZER 18: BLOW AWAY STRESS 36
    PARENTAL PERMISSION LETTER 37
    INVITATION TO JOIN GROUP 38
    STUDENT PASSES 39
    SURVEY FOR SMALL-GROUP SESSIONS 40
    EVALUATION OF GROUP SESSIONS 41
    BINGO NUMBERS 42

ANGER-MANAGEMENT 45
    SESSION 1: ANGER-MANAGEMENT 46
    SESSION 2: ANGER-MANAGEMENT 47
    SESSION 3: ANGER-MANAGEMENT 49
        ANGER 51
    SESSION 4: ANGER-MANAGEMENT 52
        KNOWING WHEN OTHERS ARE ANGRY 54
    SESSION 5: ANGER-MANAGEMENT 55
        TRIGGERS AND HOT BUTTONS 57
        STOP 58
    SESSION 6: ANGER-MANAGEMENT 59
    SESSION 7: ANGER-MANAGEMENT 61
        ANGER THERMOMETER 62
    SESSION 8: ANGER-MANAGEMENT 63
        ANGER BINGO 65
    SESSION 9: ANGER-MANAGEMENT 66

BULLYING 67
    SESSION 1: BULLYING 68
    SESSION 2: BULLYING 69
    SESSION 3: BULLYING 70
    SESSION 4: BULLYING 72
        BULLYING OR TEASING 73
    SESSION 5: BULLYING 74
        THE ROLES IN BULLYING SITUATIONS 75
    SESSION 6: BULLYING 76
        BULLYING STRATEGIES 78
    SESSION 7: BULLYING 79
        BULLY BINGO 81

COPING SKILLS 83
    SESSION 1: COPING SKILLS 84
    SESSION 2: COPING SKILLS 85
        FORMULA TO HELP YOU COPE 87
    SESSION 3: COPING SKILLS 88
        ME 89
        OTHERS 90
    SESSION 4: COPING SKILLS 91
        "I" MESSAGE/BLAMING MESSAGE 93
    SESSION 5: COPING SKILLS 94
        COMMUNICATION ROLE-PLAYS 96

SESSION 6: COPING SKILLS	97
NEGATIVE THOUGHTS ⇨ POSITIVE THOUGHTS	99
WAYS TO RAISE SELF-ESTEEM	100
SESSION 7: COPING SKILLS	101
FEELINGS SENTENCE COMPLETION	102
SESSION 8: COPING SKILLS	103
PEOPLE WHO SUPPORT ME	105
SESSION 9: COPING SKILLS	106
COPE BINGO	108

DECISION-MAKING 109

SESSION 1: DECISION-MAKING	110
SESSION 2: DECISION-MAKING	111
FIVE DECISIONS	112
SESSION 3: DECISION-MAKING	113
5 C'S IN DECISION-MAKING	115
SESSION 4: DECISION-MAKING	116
SIMPLE DECISIONS/COMPLEX DECISIONS	118
SESSION 5: DECISION-MAKING	119
WHO/WHAT INFLUENCES MY DECISIONS	120
CHOOSING THE BEST DECISION	121
SESSION 6: DECISION-MAKING	122
CAMPING TRIP	124
SESSION 7: DECISION-MAKING	125
DECISIONS I HAVE MADE	126
SESSION 8: DECISION-MAKING	127
SESSION 9: DECISION-MAKING	128
DECIDE BINGO	130

DIVORCE 131

SESSION 1: DIVORCE	132
SESSION 2: DIVORCE	133
SESSION 3: DIVORCE	134
INCOMPLETE SENTENCES	135
SESSION 4: DIVORCE	136
DIFFICULT DIVORCE CARDS	137
NOT DIFFICULT DIVORCE CARDS	138
DIFFICULT/NOT DIFFICULT SENTENCES	139
SESSION 5: DIVORCE	140
THINGS I WORRY ABOUT	141
SESSION 6: DIVORCE	142
FAMILY CHANGES	143
SESSION 7: DIVORCE	144
SECRET THOUGHTS	145
SESSION 8: DIVORCE	146
FEELINGS THERMOMETER	147
DIVORCE SITUATIONS	148
SESSION 9: DIVORCE	149
DIVORCE BINGO	151
SESSION 10: DIVORCE	152

GRIEF & LOSS 153

SESSION 1: GRIEF AND LOSS	154
SESSION 2: GRIEF AND LOSS	155
SESSION 3: GRIEF AND LOSS	156
SESSION 4: GRIEF AND LOSS	157
COLORS OF MY HEART	158
SESSION 5: GRIEF AND LOSS	159
INCOMPLETE SENTENCES FOR LOSS	160
SESSION 6: GRIEF AND LOSS	161
FAMILY CHANGES	162
SESSION 7: GRIEF AND LOSS	163
MEMORIES	164
SESSION 8: GRIEF AND LOSS	165
SESSION 9: GRIEF AND LOSS	166
THE FUNERAL	168
SESSION 10: GRIEF AND LOSS	169
MAKING MEMORIES	170
SESSION 11: GRIEF AND LOSS	171
GRIEF BINGO	173
SESSION 12: GRIEF AND LOSS	174

SELF-ESTEEM 175

SESSION 1: SELF-ESTEEM	176
SESSION 2: SELF-ESTEEM	177
SESSION 3: SELF-ESTEEM	178
MY PERSONAL CAR	179
WHOM DO YOU ADMIRE?	180
SESSION 4: SELF-ESTEEM	181
POSITIVE MIRROR	182

SESSION 5: SELF-ESTEEM 183
    ABOUT ME 185
SESSION 6: SELF-ESTEEM 186
    HOW WELL DO YOU KNOW YOURSELF? 187
SESSION 7: SELF-ESTEEM 188
    SELF-WORTH BINGO 190
SESSION 8: SELF-ESTEEM 191
    MY DREAM 192
SESSION 9: SELF-ESTEEM 193
SESSION 10: SELF-ESTEEM 194

SKILLS FOR SUCCESS 195
SESSION 1: SKILLS FOR SUCCESS 196
SESSION 2: SKILLS FOR SUCCESS 197
    SUCCESS 198
SESSION 3: SKILLS FOR SUCCESS 199
    5 C'S IN DECISION-MAKING 201
    DECISION-MAKING 202
SESSION 4: SKILLS FOR SUCCESS 203
    CHANGING NEGATIVE BELIEFS INTO POSITIVE BELIEFS 204
SESSION 5: SKILLS FOR SUCCESS 205
    TRAITS I POSSESS 206
    GOALS 207
SESSION 6: SKILLS FOR SUCCESS 208
    SPECIFIC-SUBJECT GOALS 210
SESSION 7: SKILLS FOR SUCCESS 211
    THINGS I BEGAN BUT DID NOT FINISH 213
    PRIORITY WORKSHEET 214
SESSION 8: SKILLS FOR SUCCESS 215
    RESPONSIBILITIES 217
SESSION 9: SKILLS FOR SUCCESS 218
    RESPONSIBILITY AND STUDY SKILLS 219
    SETTING GOALS FOR IMPROVEMENT 220
SESSION 10: SKILLS FOR SUCCESS 221
    GOALS BINGO 223

STRESS-MANAGEMENT 225
SESSION 1: STRESS-MANAGEMENT 226
SESSION 2: STRESS-MANAGEMENT 227
    GOOD STRESS—BAD STRESS 228
SESSION 3: STRESS-MANAGEMENT 229
    STRESS CHECKLIST 230
SESSION 4: STRESS-MANAGEMENT 231
    BODY STRESS 232
SESSION 5: STRESS-MANAGEMENT 233
    STRESS BUSTERS 234
SESSION 6: STRESS-MANAGEMENT 235
SESSION 7: STRESS-MANAGEMENT 236
SESSION 8: STRESS-MANAGEMENT 237
    STRESS BINGO 239
SESSION 9: STRESS-MANAGEMENT 240

GRAB BAG GUIDANCE 241
GRAB BAG GUIDANCE SESSIONS 242
SESSION 1: GROUP EXPECTATIONS 243
SESSION 2: GETTING TO KNOW YOU 244
    GETTING TO KNOW YOU 245
SESSION 3: ANGER-MANAGEMENT 246
    ANGER 248
SESSION 4: ANGER-MANAGEMENT BINGO 249
    ANGER BINGO 251
SESSION 5: GRIEF AND LOSS 252
SESSION 6: MORE ON GRIEF AND LOSS 253
    COLORS OF MY HEART 255
SESSION 7: GRIEF AND LOSS BINGO 256
    GRIEF BINGO 257
SESSION 8: BULLYING 258
SESSION 9: MORE ON BULLYING 259
SESSION 10: STRESS-MANAGEMENT 261
    STRESS BUSTERS 263
SESSION 11: STRESS-MANAGEMENT BINGO 264
    STRESS BINGO 265
SESSION 12: MAKE YOUR OWN STRESS BALL 266
SESSION 13: SELF-ESTEEM 267
    MY PERSONAL SHIELD 268
SESSION 14: MORE ON SELF-ESTEEM AND SELF-WORTH BINGO 269
    SELF-WORTH BINGO 271
SESSION 15: FINAL GROUP SESSION 272

DEDICATION

I dedicate this book, first to all to the wonderful students who attended Brown Middle School and participated in my groups. I think I learned as much from them as they learned from me.

I also dedicate it to two of my colleagues: Esther Burton, who was my mentor and told me that small-group counseling is an effective way to reach middle school students. Patti Grimes, school psychologist, helped me facilitate my first groups. I learned a lot from watching Patti interact with the students.

Lastly, I dedicate this to my family, who supported me in this endeavor. It has always been my dream to put these ideas in book form and share them with others. My family encouraged me to realize this dream.

INTRODUCTION

Grab Bag Guidance And Other Small-Group Counseling Topics For Middle School Students is a compilation of two types of groups:

- Specific groups focusing on a single topic
- *Grab Bag Guidance* groups that focus on several topics

The most popular of the groups is the *Grab Bag Guidance* group. In this group, students work on self-esteem, anger-management, stress-management, bullying, and loss.

Each group consists of 6-8 middle school students who meet once a week for counseling in a school setting. The students meet for approximately 7-15 weeks. The group does not meet at the same time as any academic class, but during an activity period, study hall, or non-academic class period.

Every group begins with a reading of the *Group Opening* (page 9) and the *Group Rules* (page 10). I used the ones in this book, but feel free to develop your own if they do not meet your needs. Reading the *Group Opening* and *Group Rules* at the beginning of each session reinforces what is expected of group members. Even though repeating the process at every session may seem unnecessary, it is a useful tool for keeping the group on task.

Each group begins with an *energizer*. You'll find the ones I used on pages 11-36 and identified by number within the sessions. Each group also includes a bingo game. These games are a great way to review what has been learned in previous sessions. Although the games focus on different concepts, each game requires the same numbers. Reproduce these numbers (pages 42-43) so they will be available for any group you lead from this manual.

The program also includes a sample *Parental Permission Letter* (page 37), an invitation for the students selected for the group (page 38), passes for students to use when coming to group (page 39), a *Survey For Small-Group Sessions* (page 40), and an *Evaluation Of Group Sessions* (page 41).

The activities used in these groups have worked for me and my groups. I hope they work for you, too. Enjoy!

Sincerely,

Becky Kirby

USING THE
GROUP OPENING AND *GROUP RULES*
IN GROUP SESSIONS

Each group session begins with the reading of the *Group Opening* and *Group Rules.* Students may write their own opening or you may use the *Group Opening* found on page 9. The first time the group meets, you should read the *Group Opening* and talk with the students about its meaning. Choose a different student to read the *Group Opening* at the beginning of each subsequent session.

After the *Group Opening* has been read, each student should read one of the *Group Rules.* Students may write their own rules during the first session or you may use the *Group Rules* found on page 10. At the first session, explain each rule after it is read.

Reproduce the *Group Opening* and *Group Rules* on colored cardstock and laminate them. Lamination will help the cards remain durable as they are passed from student to student at the beginning of each group.

GROUP OPENING

Our group is special.

We listen to each other and offer feedback without criticizing.

We encourage each other to participate as we work together.

We inspire and support each other.

We understand that what we say is confidential.

USING THE ENERGIZERS IN GROUP SESSIONS

Energizers are an integral part of each small-group counseling session. The energizers offered in this book have proven to work well with students. For those students who are first-time participants in a small-group counseling session, energizers are a new experience. For students who have previously participated in a small-group counseling session, the energizers may be familiar, but still effective.

In this section, you will find the energizers used with the groups. The energizers to be used in the session are identified by number.

ENERGIZER 1
INTRODUCTION

Materials Required:

For the leader:
☐ 3 *Koosh*® Balls

Preparation:

None

Energizer:

Ask the students to form a circle. Then say:

I am going to throw one ball to someone in our circle. As I toss the ball, I will say that person's name. The person who catches the ball will throw it to another person and say that person's name. These two group members will continue to throw the ball back and forth to each other as they call out each other's name.

Since this may seem easy to you, I am going to add two more balls to the game. A few seconds after I have tossed the first ball, I will toss the second ball to another group member. The person catching the ball will then toss it to someone not already playing the game and say that person's name. These two group members will continue to throw the ball back and forth to each other as they call out each other's name.

A few seconds later, I will toss the third ball to one of the remaining two group members. These two group members will continue to throw the ball back and forth to each other as they call out each other's name. The balls will be going in all directions. Remember: Each time you catch the ball, you must throw it to the same person, while saying his or her name.

Using three Koosh balls, begin the activity. You may increase or reduce the speed at which the balls are tossed, in keeping with the students' ability. Set a time limit for the activity. When the allotted time has elapsed, ask someone in the group to name everyone in the group. (*Note:* Each person may take a turn naming everyone in the group.)

Alternate Idea:

Instead of having each student throw the ball to the same person, group members may toss the ball to any person in the circle. Each person may have only one ball at a time.

ENERGIZER 2
LISTENING GAME

Materials Required:

For the leader:
- ☐ *Listening Skill Cards* (pages 16-21)
- ☐ Chalkboard and chalk, chart paper and marker, or dry-erase board and marker

Preparation:

Reproduce the *Listening Skill Cards* on same-color paper. If possible, laminate the cards for durability.

Energizer:

Involve the students in the following listening game. The purpose of this game is to impress upon the students the importance of being good listeners during group sessions.

Write the letters **LISTEN** on the board. Then say:

Look at the word written on the board. Scramble the letters to spell another word that uses each of the letters on the board.

Pause for the students' responses. When they say the word *silent*, say:

These two words go together, because when you listen, you are silent.

Show the students the six *Listening Skill Cards*. Good listening skills are printed on three of the cards. Poor listening skills are printed on the other three. Review these cards with the students.

The good listening skills are:

Focus—Look at the person who is talking. Be aware of your body language. You may lean forward a bit as you listen.

Accept—Nod or smile. Say "uh, uh" to let the person know you are listening and accepting what he/she is saying.

Give Feedback—This is when you may agree or disagree with what a person is saying. You may ask questions at this time. You must stay on the subject.

The poor listening skills are:

Interrupt—Talking or making noise interrupts someone who is talking.

Change The Subject—This is just what it says. If someone is talking about a vacation and you say, "I can't wait to get home tonight. We're having spaghetti for dinner," that is *changing the subject*.

Ignore—Doing something else when someone is talking or looking away from the person who is talking.

Introduce the *Listening Game* to the students by saying:

Open-ended questions give others an opportunity to respond to you. These questions may begin with "What" or "Tell me about." A closed question requires a one- or two-word answer like "yes" or "no." For the purpose of our game, you will ask open-ended questions.

In this game, one group member will hold a card above someone's head without letting any of the other group members see what is written on the card.

The student holding the card will then ask the student over whose head the card is being held an open-ended question such as: "What are you doing this weekend?" As the person responds, the student holding the card will role-play the skill printed on it.

Everyone in the group should try to guess which skill the student is role-playing and whether it is a good or poor listening skill. When someone guesses correctly, the person over whose head the card was held selects a new card and group member, and asks him or her an open-ended question.

Make sure every group member has a turn presenting this energizer.

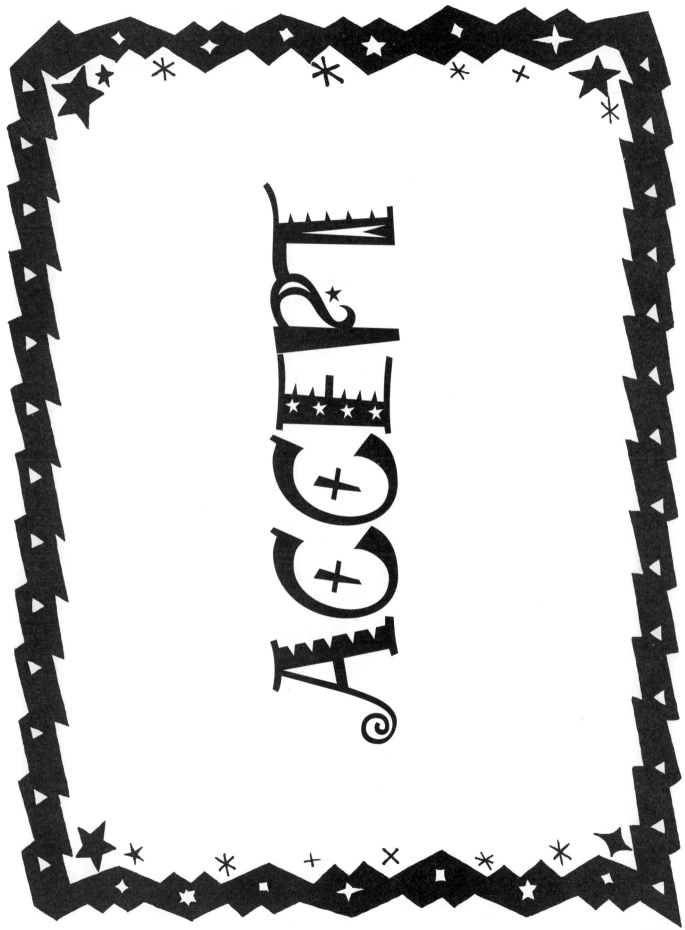

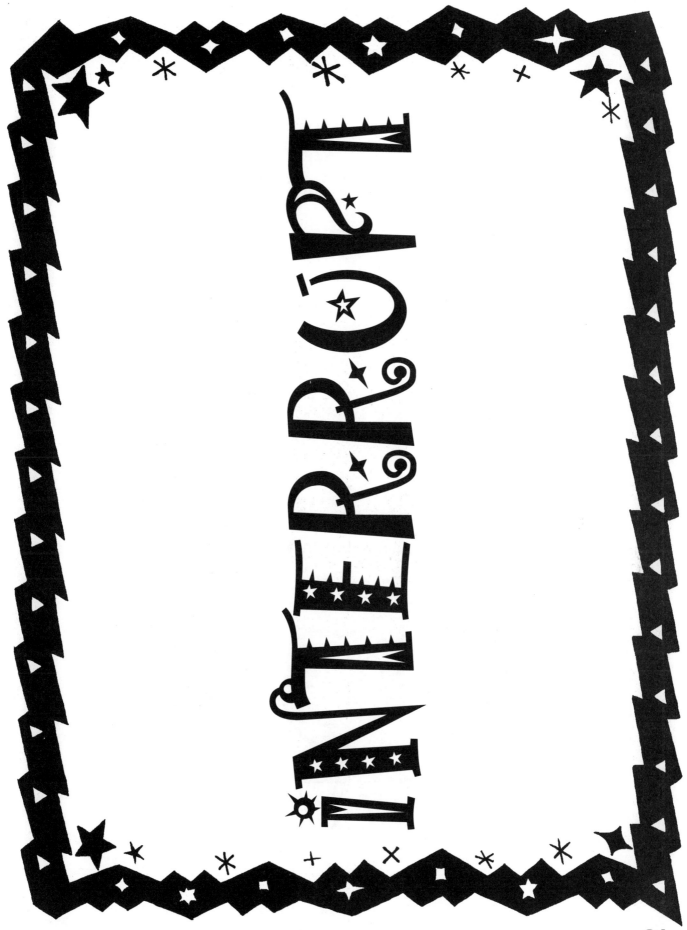

ENERGIZER 3
TELLING ABOUT YOURSELF

Materials Required:

For the leader:
☐ Package of m & m's® or Skittles® candy

Preparation:

None

Energizer:

Have the students pass the candy around the group. Say:

Take more than one piece of candy, but no more than 10 pieces.

After everyone in the group has taken some candy, say:

For each piece of candy you have taken, tell us one thing about yourself. I will go first.

After modeling the activity, have the students take turns telling the group things about themselves.

22   GRAB BAG GUIDANCE © 2005 MAR*CO PRODUCTS, INC. 1-800-448-2197

ENERGIZER 4
FEELINGS CUBE

Materials Required:

For the leader:
- ☐ Empty square box like one a mug would come in
- ☐ Black marker
- ☐ Contact paper or pastel paint and paintbrush

Preparation:

Cover the square box with contact paper or paint it white or a pastel color. Let the paint dry thoroughly. Using the marker, write the following words on the cube:

- Frightened
- Miserable
- Frustrated
- Blissful
- Surprised
- Disappointed

Energizer:

Ask the students to form a circle. Then say:

Each student will take a turn rolling the Feelings Cube into the center of the circle. Look at the word showing on the top of the cube, then describe a time you had that feeling.

If the student cannot think of anything to say, allow him/her to roll the cube again.

Feelings Cube For Divorce Group:

Follow the previous directions, but change the words on the cube. For a Divorce Group, write the following words:

- Problems
- Changes
- Legal worries
- Step-families
- Parents' new partners
- Caught in the middle

Feelings Cube For Self-Esteem Group:

Follow the previous directions, but change the words on the cube. For a Self-Esteem Group, write the following words:

- I like …
- I am pleased with …
- Others like me because …
- I am a good friend because …
- My favorite place is …
- My best friend is …

ENERGIZER 5
SENTENCE STRIPS

Materials Required:

For the leader:
- ☐ *Sentence Strips* (below)
- ☐ Scissors
- ☐ Basket

Preparation:

Make a copy of the *Sentence Strips*. Cut the strips apart and place them in the basket.

Energizer:

Introduce the activity by saying:

I am going to pass this basket to each of you. The basket contains Sentence Strips. *When the basket comes to you, pull out a* Sentence Strip *and answer it. If you can't answer it, you may put it back into the basket and draw another one. Hold onto your* Sentence Strip *until all the sentences that were in the basket have been completed. Then I will collect the* Sentence Strips.

| What takes too long? |
| What made you angry recently? |
| If I were principal of this school, I would … |
| In my free time, I like to … |
| I worry about … |
| What would make me happy now is … |
| My favorite place is … |
| Three things I would like others to say about me are … |
| A time a friend helped me out was … |

ENERGIZER 6
FEELING CARDS

Materials Required:

For the leader:
- ☐ *Feelings Cards* (pages 25-29)
- ☐ Scissors

Preparation:

Make a copy of the *Feelings Cards* and cut them apart. If possible, laminate the cards for durability.

Energizer:

Place the *Feeling Cards* throughout the room. Then say:

Choose two or three cards that show how you are feeling today.

Once everyone has chosen cards, have the students discuss why they chose the *Feeling Cards* they did.

★ RELAXED	BETRAYED
GRAB BAG GUIDANCE: FEELINGS CARDS © 2005 MAR*CO PRODUCTS, INC. 1-800-448-2197	GRAB BAG GUIDANCE: FEELINGS CARDS © 2005 MAR*CO PRODUCTS, INC. 1-800-448-2197
CONFIDENT	JEALOUS
GRAB BAG GUIDANCE: FEELINGS CARDS © 2005 MAR*CO PRODUCTS, INC. 1-800-448-2197	GRAB BAG GUIDANCE: FEELINGS CARDS © 2005 MAR*CO PRODUCTS, INC. 1-800-448-2197

☆ HAPPY	ANGRY
GRAB BAG GUIDANCE: FEELINGS CARDS © 2005 MAR✶CO PRODUCTS, INC. 1-800-448-2197	*GRAB BAG GUIDANCE: FEELINGS CARDS* © 2005 MAR✶CO PRODUCTS, INC. 1-800-448-2197
ANNOYED	OVERWORKED
GRAB BAG GUIDANCE: FEELINGS CARDS © 2005 MAR✶CO PRODUCTS, INC. 1-800-448-2197	*GRAB BAG GUIDANCE: FEELINGS CARDS* © 2005 MAR✶CO PRODUCTS, INC. 1-800-448-2197
CALM	DISCOURAGED
GRAB BAG GUIDANCE: FEELINGS CARDS © 2005 MAR✶CO PRODUCTS, INC. 1-800-448-2197	*GRAB BAG GUIDANCE: FEELINGS CARDS* © 2005 MAR✶CO PRODUCTS, INC. 1-800-448-2197
DISAPPOINTED	HOPEFUL ☆
GRAB BAG GUIDANCE: FEELINGS CARDS © 2005 MAR✶CO PRODUCTS, INC. 1-800-448-2197	*GRAB BAG GUIDANCE: FEELINGS CARDS* © 2005 MAR✶CO PRODUCTS, INC. 1-800-448-2197
EXCITED ☆	ECSTATIC
GRAB BAG GUIDANCE: FEELINGS CARDS © 2005 MAR✶CO PRODUCTS, INC. 1-800-448-2197	*GRAB BAG GUIDANCE: FEELINGS CARDS* © 2005 MAR✶CO PRODUCTS, INC. 1-800-448-2197

SAD *GRAB BAG GUIDANCE: FEELINGS CARDS* © 2005 MAR✶CO PRODUCTS, INC. 1-800-448-2197	**MISERABLE** *GRAB BAG GUIDANCE: FEELINGS CARDS* © 2005 MAR✶CO PRODUCTS, INC. 1-800-448-2197
SATISFIED *GRAB BAG GUIDANCE: FEELINGS CARDS* © 2005 MAR✶CO PRODUCTS, INC. 1-800-448-2197	 **PROUD** *GRAB BAG GUIDANCE: FEELINGS CARDS* © 2005 MAR✶CO PRODUCTS, INC. 1-800-448-2197
SURPRISED *GRAB BAG GUIDANCE: FEELINGS CARDS* © 2005 MAR✶CO PRODUCTS, INC. 1-800-448-2197	**INTERESTED** *GRAB BAG GUIDANCE: FEELINGS CARDS* © 2005 MAR✶CO PRODUCTS, INC. 1-800-448-2197
SCATTERED *GRAB BAG GUIDANCE: FEELINGS CARDS* © 2005 MAR✶CO PRODUCTS, INC. 1-800-448-2197	**BORED** *GRAB BAG GUIDANCE: FEELINGS CARDS* © 2005 MAR✶CO PRODUCTS, INC. 1-800-448-2197
 **SILLY** *GRAB BAG GUIDANCE: FEELINGS CARDS* © 2005 MAR✶CO PRODUCTS, INC. 1-800-448-2197	**LOVING** *GRAB BAG GUIDANCE: FEELINGS CARDS* © 2005 MAR✶CO PRODUCTS, INC. 1-800-448-2197

IMPORTANT	INTELLIGENT
GRAB BAG GUIDANCE: FEELINGS CARDS © 2005 MAR★CO PRODUCTS, INC. 1-800-448-2197	*GRAB BAG GUIDANCE: FEELINGS CARDS* © 2005 MAR★CO PRODUCTS, INC. 1-800-448-2197
★ TENSE	CONTENT
GRAB BAG GUIDANCE: FEELINGS CARDS © 2005 MAR★CO PRODUCTS, INC. 1-800-448-2197	*GRAB BAG GUIDANCE: FEELINGS CARDS* © 2005 MAR★CO PRODUCTS, INC. 1-800-448-2197
ANXIOUS	WORRIED
GRAB BAG GUIDANCE: FEELINGS CARDS © 2005 MAR★CO PRODUCTS, INC. 1-800-448-2197	*GRAB BAG GUIDANCE: FEELINGS CARDS* © 2005 MAR★CO PRODUCTS, INC. 1-800-448-2197
ENERGETIC	PEACEFUL
GRAB BAG GUIDANCE: FEELINGS CARDS © 2005 MAR★CO PRODUCTS, INC. 1-800-448-2197	*GRAB BAG GUIDANCE: FEELINGS CARDS* © 2005 MAR★CO PRODUCTS, INC. 1-800-448-2197
NERVOUS	CONFUSED
GRAB BAG GUIDANCE: FEELINGS CARDS © 2005 MAR★CO PRODUCTS, INC. 1-800-448-2197	*GRAB BAG GUIDANCE: FEELINGS CARDS* © 2005 MAR★CO PRODUCTS, INC. 1-800-448-2197

FRUSTRATED *GRAB BAG GUIDANCE: FEELINGS CARDS* © 2005 MAR✶CO PRODUCTS, INC. 1-800-448-2197	**LONELY** *GRAB BAG GUIDANCE: FEELINGS CARDS* © 2005 MAR✶CO PRODUCTS, INC. 1-800-448-2197
DIFFERENT *GRAB BAG GUIDANCE: FEELINGS CARDS* © 2005 MAR✶CO PRODUCTS, INC. 1-800-448-2197	**OVERWHELMED** *GRAB BAG GUIDANCE: FEELINGS CARDS* © 2005 MAR✶CO PRODUCTS, INC. 1-800-448-2197
EXHAUSTED *GRAB BAG GUIDANCE: FEELINGS CARDS* © 2005 MAR✶CO PRODUCTS, INC. 1-800-448-2197	**SUPPORTED** *GRAB BAG GUIDANCE: FEELINGS CARDS* © 2005 MAR✶CO PRODUCTS, INC. 1-800-448-2197
★ **JOYFUL** *GRAB BAG GUIDANCE: FEELINGS CARDS* © 2005 MAR✶CO PRODUCTS, INC. 1-800-448-2197	**UNSUPPORTED** *GRAB BAG GUIDANCE: FEELINGS CARDS* © 2005 MAR✶CO PRODUCTS, INC. 1-800-448-2197
ORGANIZED *GRAB BAG GUIDANCE: FEELINGS CARDS* © 2005 MAR✶CO PRODUCTS, INC. 1-800-448-2197	**UNDECIDED** *GRAB BAG GUIDANCE: FEELINGS CARDS* © 2005 MAR✶CO PRODUCTS, INC. 1-800-448-2197

ENERGIZER 7
SNOWBALL FUN

Materials Required:

For each student:
- ☐ *Open-Ended Sentences* (below)
- ☐ Pencil

Preparation:

Make a copy of *Open-Ended Sentences* for each student.

Energizer:

Give each group member a copy of the *Open-Ended Sentences* and a pencil. Then say:

Do not write your name on this paper. Complete the sentences. When you have finished, wad the paper up like a snowball. When I say, "Begin," throw the wads of paper around, being careful not to hit anyone. When I say, "Stop," pick up one of the snowballs. Taking turns, each of you will read what is written on the snowball you chose and try to guess who wrote it.

Begin the activity.

OPEN-ENDED SENTENCES

My favorite activity is _____

_____.

Something you don't know about me is _____

_____

_____.

My favorite place is _____

_____.

ENERGIZER 8
YARN BALL REVIEW

Materials Required:

For the leader:
☐ Ball of yarn

Preparation:

None

Energizer:

Holding one end of a ball of yarn, tell the students:

While holding the end of the strand, I will toss the ball of yarn to a member of the group. When you catch the ball of yarn, describe something about bullying (or how to handle anger, or that will help you do better in school) that you learned in group. Then, holding onto a piece of the yarn, call out a person's name and toss the ball of yarn to him or her.

The person catching the ball of yarn will continue the game by describing what he or she has learned, call out another name, and throw the ball of yarn while holding onto the strand.

We will continue the game until everyone has had a turn and every group member is holding onto a piece of the yarn. This creates a web.

ENERGIZER 9
TRUTH OR LIE?

Materials Required:

None

Preparation:

None

Energizer:

Introduce the activity by saying:

You are going to tell the group three things about yourself. Two of the things you will say are true, and the other will be a lie.

After you describe each thing, each student in the group will signify which statement he or she believes is a lie by holding up one, two, or three fingers.

For example:

If you think the first statement is a lie, hold up one finger.

If you think the second statement is a lie, hold up two fingers.

If you think the third statement is a lie, hold up three fingers.

Think of the three things you want to say to the group. (Pause for the students to decide what to say.) *Let's begin.*

ENERGIZER 10
SOMETHING I LIKED

Materials Required:

For the leader:
- ☐ Rainstick or similar item

Preparation:

None

Energizer:

Introduce the activity by saying:

> *The rainstick will be passed from person to person in the group. When it is passed to you, talk about something you have enjoyed about being in the group.*

Decision-Making Group:

Pass the rainstick (or something similar) from person to person in the group. Have the students tell one thing they have learned about decision-making.

Skills For Success Group:

Pass the rainstick (or something similar) from person to person in the group. Have the students describe one responsibility that they fulfilled this past week.

ENERGIZER 11
STRENGTHS

Materials Required:

None

Preparation:

None

Energizer:

Have the students stand in a straight line, one right behind the other. Then say:

> *Think of two of your strengths which you are willing to share with the members of this group. The first person in line will turn and tell the second person in line his or her two strengths. Then the first person will go to the end of the line. The original second person, who is now the first person in line, repeats the process. This process continues until everyone in the group has had a turn to describe his or her strengths.*

ENERGIZER 12
DECISION-MAKING

Materials Required:

None

Preparation:

None

Energizer:

Ask the students to stand up. Designate opposite areas of the room for the students to stand, depending upon their answers. As you read each of the statements below, the students should go to the side of the room that best describes them. Begin each statement with:

Do you prefer ...

> hamburgers or hot dogs
> pizza or nachos
> red or blue
> science or social studies
> baseball or football
> independence or dependence
> bananas or oranges
> rain or snow
> dogs or cats
> SUVs or sports cars
> walking or running

Discuss the students' answers. Talk about whether the choices were easy or difficult to make.

ENERGIZER 13
LIKENESS LETTER

Materials Required:

None

Preparation:

None

Energizer:

Instruct the students to sit in a circle. Then go around the circle and have each student say his/her name and something he/she likes that begins with the first letter of the name. For example:

> "My name is Anne and I like apples."

As the activity progresses around the circle, each person must repeat everything that has already been said, including everyone's names and preferences. When the last person has participated, the first person must repeat everyone's name and preference.

Alternate Idea:

The activity can be made more difficult by having students give their first and last names and say something they like that begins with the first letter of the first name and something they like that begins with the last letter of the last name.

ENERGIZER 14
A BROKEN HEART

Materials Required:

For the leader:
- ☐ Art paper
- ☐ Marker
- ☐ Scissors

Preparation:

Using the marker, draw a large heart on the piece of art paper. Cut the heart into the number of pieces equal to the number of students in the group.

Energizer:

Give each student a piece of the heart. Then ask:

Why do you think each of you has received a piece of the heart? (Most students will answer that someone who loses someone, might say his/her heart is broken.)

As a group, put the heart together. Then say:

As people go through the grief process, the pieces of the heart go back together as they accept their loss and move forward.

ENERGIZER 15
ESCALATOR

Materials Required:

None

Preparation:

None

Energizer:

Tell the students they have three choices. They may pretend they are going up an escalator to one of two places or choose to stay where they are in the room. If they go up the escalator, they may go up one floor, get off, and visit with a friend or they may go to another floor, get off, and arrive at their favorite place. Give the students a few minutes to decide where they want to be.

Have the students close their eyes and, if pretending they are not staying where they are, envision stepping onto the up escalator. Then they should envision getting off on the floor they want to visit—either with a friend or at their favorite place.

Allow two or three minutes for the students to experience their choice. During that time, there should be no talking and the students' eyes should remain closed. When the allotted time has elapsed, tell the students to think about saying "good-bye," and stepping onto the down escalator. When they reach the ground floor, they may open their eyes.

Discuss where each person went, what happened, and whatever else the students feel comfortable sharing about the experience. Tell the students that when they feel stressed, this is one way they can try to relieve tension.

ENERGIZER 16
A TO Z STORY

Materials Required:

None

Preparation:

None

Energizer:

Go around the group and have the students make up a story, with each person using the next letter of the alphabet to add the next line.

Example:

A girl

belonged to a

chorus group called

dandelions and sheets …

Going from A–Z, finish the story.

ENERGIZER 17
PEOPLE/POSSESSIONS

Materials Required:

For each student:
- ☐ Paper
- ☐ Pencil

Preparation:

None

Energizer:

Give each student a piece of paper and pencil. Have the students divide the paper in half lengthwise and label one side *People* and the other side *Possessions*. Then say:

> *A volcano is going to erupt and destroy the area in which you live. You are allowed to take 20 people and 20 things with you. List in each column the people and things you would take.*

When the students have completed their lists, have them share their choices. Take note of the people and things that are important in their lives.

ENERGIZER 18
BLOW AWAY STRESS

Materials Required:

For the leader:
- ☐ Soap solution for bubbles

For each student:
- ☐ Bubble wand

Preparation

None

Energizer

Have the students think about what is causing stress in their lives and pretend to put those things inside the bubbles.

As the students blow the stress-filled bubbles, tell them to think about their stresses leaving them as the bubbles float way and disappear.

Date _____

Dear Parent or Guardian,

Your child has volunteered/been chosen to participate in a small-group counseling session. I will facilitate the group, which will last 7-15 weeks and meet once a week during a non-academic class period. The group is called _____ .

One of my goals as a middle school counselor is to meet with as many students as possible. I hope to accomplish this through students' participation in small-group counseling sessions.

Please complete the slip below, giving permission for your child to participate in the group. Have your child return it to me as soon as possible.

If you have any questions, you may call me at (____) - _____ - _____ , extension _____ .

Sincerely,

School Counselor

Please fill out, detach, and have your child return the portion below to the school counselor by _____ .

Your Child's Name: _____

has my permission to participate in small-group counseling sessions for _____ . I understand that the group will meet once a week during a non-academic class period. The group will last 7-15 weeks.

_____
(Parent or Guardian's Signature)

YOU'RE INVITED!

You are invited to participate in small-group counseling sessions with _____, your school counselor.

We will meet on:

_____, during _____.
DAY OF THE WEEK   PERIOD

Our first session will be on _____ at _____.
                                    DATE   TIME

The name of the group is _____.

I am looking forward to having you in our group!

☆ _____
              SIGNATURE

TO SMALL-GROUP
SESSION

Please excuse

_____

from class

Date _____

Period _____

TO SMALL-GROUP
SESSION

Please excuse

_____

from class

Date _____

Period _____

TO SMALL-GROUP
SESSION

Please excuse

_____

from class

Date _____

Period _____

TO SMALL-GROUP
SESSION

Please excuse

_____

from class

Date _____

Period _____

GRAB BAG GUIDANCE © 2005 MAR✶CO PRODUCTS, INC. 1-800-448-2197

SURVEY
FOR SMALL-GROUP SESSIONS

Small-group counseling sessions will take place once a week during one non-academic class period. The group will meet for approximately 7-15 weeks. If you are interested in participating in one of these groups, please mark your choices below.

Please mark 1 for your first choice, 2 for your second choice, and 3 for your third choice. Return this form to the guidance office after you complete it.

- ☐ Anger-Management
- ☐ Bullying
- ☐ Coping Skills
- ☐ Decision-Making
- ☐ Divorce
- ☐ Loss (Grief)
- ☐ Self-Esteem
- ☐ Skills For Success
- ☐ Stress-Management
- ☐ Grab Bag (includes sessions on anger-management, loss, stress, bullying, and self-esteem)

Name_____

Grade _____ Homeroom _____

EVALUATION
OF GROUP SESSIONS

1.	Did you look forward to coming to group?	YES	NO
2.	Did the day and time work well for you?	YES	NO
3.	Did you form any new friendships from being in group?	YES	NO
4.	Have you applied any of the new skills you learned in group?	YES	NO
5.	If so, did you have success with the new skill(s)?	YES	NO
6.	Have you changed any behavior since you have been in group?	YES	NO
7.	Did you feel like you were listened to in group?	YES	NO
8.	Did you feel like you could trust the group members?	YES	NO
9.	Was it difficult to make up work you missed while attending group?	YES	NO
10.	Would you want to be in another group?	YES	NO
11.	Would you recommend being in a group to your friends?	YES	NO

12. On a scale of 1-10, with 1 being the lowest and 10 being the highest, how would you rate your experience in this group? _____

PLEASE FEEL FREE TO ADD ADDITIONAL COMMENTS

Thank you for participating in our group!

BINGO NUMBERS

1	2	3	4	5
6	7	8	9	10
11	12	13	14	15
16	17	18	19	20
21	22	23	24	25
26	27	28	29	30
31	32	33	34	35
36	37	38	39	40

41	42	43	44	45
46	47	48	49	50
51	52	53	54	55
56	57	58	59	60
61	62	63	64	65
66	67	68	69	70
71	72	73	74	75

ANGER MANAGEMENT

SESSION 1
ANGER-MANAGEMENT

Purpose:

To introduce group members to each other, explain the purpose of the group, and emphasize the importance of good listening skills

Materials Required:

For the leader:
- ☐ *Group Opening* (page 9)
- ☐ *Group Rules* (page 10)
- ☐ Materials for *Energizer 1* (page 13)
- ☐ Materials for *Energizer 2* (page 14)

For each student:
- ☐ 2-pocket manila folder
- ☐ Crayons or markers
- ☐ Pencil

Preparation:

If you have not already done so, reproduce the *Group Rules* and *Group Opening*. Laminate the pages if possible.

Read the instructions for *Energizer 1* and *Energizer 2*. Gather and prepare the necessary materials.

Session Content:

- Introduce the *Group Rules* and the *Group Opening* to the students.

- Present *Energizer 1*.

- Present *Energizer 2*.

- Give each student a folder, crayons or markers, and a pencil. Tell the students the folders will be used to hold their handouts.

- Instruct the students to write their name on the folder, along with the day and class period the group meets. Allow time for the students to use the crayons or markers to decorate their folders.

- Explain to the students that the purpose of the group is to explore the causes of anger and ways to react to anger-provoking situations in a healthy manner.

- Collect the folders. (*Note:* The folders will be collected by the leader at the end of each session. At the final session, the students may keep whatever they want from their folders. Shred anything the students do not want to keep.)

SESSION 2
ANGER-MANAGEMENT

Purpose:

To identify words, physical feelings, and results associated with anger

Materials Required:

For the leader:
- ☐ *Group Opening* (page 9)
- ☐ *Group Rules* (page 10)
- ☐ Materials for *Energizer 4* (page 23)
- ☐ Chalkboard and chalk or dry erase board and marker
- ☐ Chart paper
- ☐ Marker
- ☐ Masking tape

For each student:
- ☐ Marker

Preparation:

Read the instructions for *Energizer 4*. Gather and prepare the necessary materials.

Label three sheets of chart paper:

1. Words Associated With Anger
2. Where You Physically Feel Anger
3. Results Of Being Angry

Attach the charts to the wall with masking tape.

Session Content:

- Select a student to read the *Group Opening*.

- Pass the *Group Rules* around. Have each student read one rule aloud until all of the rules have been read.

- Present *Energizer 4*.

- Write the letters ANGER on the board. Then say:

    Anger is only one letter away from **danger**.

    Add the letter D to the front of ANGER to spell DANGER. Then say:

    Everyone gets angry. What is important is how you handle your anger. Anger is an emotion, not a behavior. Aggression is a behavior and aggression often gives anger a bad name.

- Give each student a marker. Then continue the session by saying:

    There are three pieces of chart paper hanging on the wall. Look at the chart paper labeled Words Associated With Anger. *Think of all the words you associate with anger. Go to the wall and write those words on the chart paper.*

    Examples of words associated with anger could be:

    Aggressive
    Hurt
    Mad
    Blaming
    Sad
    Defiant

- Review the list and talk about the ways people feel when they are angry. Then say:

    Next, I want you to think about how you feel when you are angry. Look at the chart paper labeled Where You Physically Feel Anger. *Think of all the words that describe how your body may feel when you are angry. Go to the wall and write your ideas on the chart paper.*

  Examples of physical responses to anger could be:

    Heart beats faster
    Hands get sweaty
    Mouth tightens
    Fists clench

- Discuss the students' suggestions. Then say:

    Finally, I want you to think of the different results that could occur depending on how people handle their anger. Go to the chart labeled Results Of Being Angry *and write your ideas on it.*

  Examples of results of anger could be:

    Physical violence
    Getting into trouble at home
    Getting into trouble at school
    Losing friends

- Discuss what the students have written on the chart.

- Review all three lists. Tell the students that at the next session, the group will review the rules for handling anger.

SESSION 3
ANGER-MANAGEMENT

Purpose:

To have the students identify ways they react to anger-provoking situations

Materials Required:

For the leader:
- ☐ *Group Opening* (page 9)
- ☐ *Group Rules* (page 10)
- ☐ Materials for *Energizer 3* (page 22)
- ☐ Chalkboard and chalk or dry-erase board and marker

For each student:
- ☐ Student's folder
- ☐ *Anger* (page 51)
- ☐ Pencil

Preparation:

Read the instructions for *Energizer 3*. Gather the necessary materials.

Make a copy of *Anger* for each student.

Session Content:

- Give each student his/her folder.

- Select a student to read the *Group Opening*.

- Pass the *Group Rules* around. Have each student read one rule aloud until all of the rules have been read.

- Present *Energizer 3*.

- Give each student a copy of *Anger* and a pencil. Then say:

  Look at the first statement on your activity sheet. Think of three different ways you act when you are angry. Remember: People don't always handle anger the same way. Sometimes they may yell, other times, cry. At times, they may want to talk with someone.

- Have the students complete the first section of the *Anger* activity sheet. Then review the other statements on the activity sheet, answer any questions the students may ask, and have them complete the activity sheet.

- Continue the session by saying:

  I am going to list some of the ways you and I handle anger.

  On the board, write three ways you handle anger. Then have the students name the ways to handle anger that they wrote on the *Anger* activity sheet. Add their suggestions to the list.

  Then say:

  Now I am going to add to this list. I am going to add ideas about how other students handle anger. Some ideas will suggest healthy ways to handle anger. Others will suggest unhealthy ways of handling anger. If you know of ways people handle anger that are not listed on the board, raise your hand and tell us what they are. I will add them to our list.

Below are some examples of what students often say:

cry	talk with someone
yell	go to my bedroom
hit	kick
read	write
throw things	punch something
draw	leave
call a friend	take a walk
eat	jog
exercise	spread rumors
play sports	drive fast
watch TV	break things
count to 10	play videogames

- Once the list is complete, tell the students:

  These are three rules about handling anger.

  1. *Don't hurt yourself.*
  2. *Don't hurt anyone else.*
  3. *Don't damage or destroy property.*

- Have the students cross out suggestions on the list that might hurt them or someone else and the suggestions that might damage or destroy property. Circle the other suggestions.

- Tell the students:

  Look at the suggestions that are circled. These are healthy ways of handling anger. When we are angry, each of us can chose to react in a healthy or unhealthy manner.

- Label the chart *Healthy And Unhealthy Reactions To Anger.* Save this chart for the next session.

- Discuss the remaining statements on the *Anger* activity sheet.

- Have the students put their activity sheets in their folders. Collect the folders.

ANGER

Three ways I act when I am angry are:

1. _____
2. _____
3. _____

I get angry when my mom _____
_____.

I get angry when my dad _____
_____.

I get angry when my best friend _____
_____.

I get angry when my teacher _____
_____.

If other people saw me when I am angry, they would _____
_____.

Five things, other than people, that make me angry are:

1. _____
2. _____
3. _____
4. _____
5. _____

SESSION 4
ANGER-MANAGEMENT

Purpose:

To have the students recognize when others are angry and analyze their own reactions to anger

Materials Required:

For the leader:
- ☐ *Group Opening* (page 9)
- ☐ *Group Rules* (page 10)
- ☐ Materials for *Energizer 5* (page 24)
- ☐ Chart of *Unhealthy And Healthy Reactions To Anger* from Session #3

For each student:
- ☐ Student's folder
- ☐ *Knowing When Others Are Angry* (page 54)
- ☐ Pencil

Preparation:

Read the instructions for *Energizer 5*. Gather and prepare the necessary materials.

Make a copy of *Knowing When Others Are Angry* for each student.

Session Content:

- Give each student his/her folder.

- Select a student to read the *Group Opening*.

- Pass the *Group Rules* around. Have each student read one rule aloud until all of the rules have been read.

- Present *Energizer 5*.

- Give each student a copy of *Knowing When Others Are Angry* and a pencil. Then say:

    Think about what you notice when someone is angry. How do you know that person is angry? Write your answers in the four squares on your activity sheet. When you have completed the activity sheet, we will discuss your conclusions.

- Discuss what the students wrote about each topic. Then divide the students into pairs and say:

    Discuss with your partner:

    Something that made you angry.

    What took place before you got angry.

    How your body reacted when you were angry.

    Tell the students how much time they have for their discussions.

- When the allotted time has elapsed, say:

    It is important to pay attention to our bodies when we are angry. In our last session, we listed different ways that people show they are angry.

Let's see how many you can remember. Very quickly, name all the ways you can remember that people show they are angry.

Allow about two minutes for the students to name ways that people show they are angry.

- Continue the session by saying:

    When you are angry, you may find yourself out of control, holding in your feelings, feeling very excited, or reacting in other ways. If the reactions you experience upset you or make you feel sick, it is important for you to recognize those reactions so you can do something to change the situation.

    I would like you to brainstorm about ways people can get out of a situation in which someone else is angry and trying to pull them into the anger-provoking situation.

    Examples may include:

    Making an excuse
    Using humor
    Getting help

- Conclude the session by reminding the students of the three rules about handling anger:

    1. Don't hurt yourself.
    2. Don't hurt others.
    3. Don't damage or destroy property.

- Using the *Unhealthy And Healthy Reactions To Anger* chart, review the healthy ways to handle anger that were mentioned in the last session.

- Have the students put their activity sheets in their folders. Collect the folders.

KNOWING WHEN OTHERS ARE ANGRY

HOW DO YOU KNOW WHEN SOMEONE IS ANGRY?

HOW DOES THAT PERSON'S BODY LOOK?

HOW DOES THAT PERSON'S FACE LOOK?

IF THE PERSON DIDN'T TALK, HOW WOULD YOU KNOW THAT HE/SHE IS ANGRY?

SESSION 5
ANGER-MANAGEMENT

Purpose:

To identify what "triggers" each student to become angry and positive ways to handle anger

Materials Required:

For the leader:
- ☐ *Group Opening* (page 9)
- ☐ *Group Rules* (page 10)
- ☐ Materials for *Energizer 8* (page 31)
- ☐ Koosh® ball
- ☐ Chalkboard and chalk or dry-erase board and marker

For each student:
- ☐ Student's folder
- ☐ *Triggers And Hot Buttons* (page 57)
- ☐ *Stop* (page 58)
- ☐ Pencil

Preparation:

Read the instructions for *Energizer 8*. Gather the necessary materials. (*Note:* In this energizer, the students should tell one thing they can do to handle anger.)

Make a copy of *Triggers And Hot Buttons* and *Stop* for each student.

Session Content:

- Give each student his/her folder.

- Select a student to read the *Group Opening*.

- Pass the *Group Rules* around. Have each student read one rule aloud until all of the rules have been read.

- Present *Energizer 8*.

- Tell the students:

    Triggers and hot buttons are things that happen or that people say that make you angry. Every person is different. Something one person can handle might make another person angry.

- Ask the students to stand in two lines facing each other. Give one student the Koosh ball. Then say:

    The person holding the ball will name something that makes him or her angry, then toss the ball to someone else. The person catching the ball will say what makes him or her angry, then toss the ball to another student. Continue tossing the ball until everyone has had a turn. I will record your responses on the board.

    Begin the activity. Have the students toss the ball until everyone has had a turn to name something that makes him/her angry.

- Continue the session by saying:

    Something I have written on the board may be your triggers or hot buttons. These are things that you know will make you angry. It is important to be aware of your triggers or hot buttons, because they may cause you trouble.

Let's think about triggers and hot buttons for a few minutes. Think about a situation that made you angry. Tell us what happened. What led up to the situation? What were your triggers or hot buttons?

Have the students share their answers.

- Continue the session by saying:

    Once you know what triggers your anger or pushes your hot buttons, there are some preventative measures you can take. You can use self-talk to calm yourself down. Think of things you can say to calm yourself and write them on the board.

    Examples of preventative self-talk are:

    I am upset, but I can handle it.

    Stay calm.

    It is not worth the consequences.

- After the students have written their self-talk statements on the board, say:

    Self-talk is only one way to handle triggers or hot buttons. Some other ways are:

    − Get out of the situation— make an excuse, use humor, get help.

    − Picture a stop sign. Stop and think before you react.

    − Use an "I" Message to let the person know how you feel. An example of an "I" Message would be:

    *When __ happens,
    I feel _____,
    because _____ .*

    "I" Messages are effective because the person cannot argue with how you feel. Make sure your message does not sound like you are blaming the other person.

- Give each student a copy of *Triggers And Hot Buttons* and a pencil. Review the directions. Then have the students complete the activity sheet. When everyone has finished, have the students share their thoughts with the group.

- Say to the students:

    In today's lesson, we have learned ways to handle our triggers or hot buttons. We have learned about self-talk, removing ourselves from the situation, and "I" Messages. We also learned about stopping and thinking before reacting. I have a Stop sign for each of you. It will remind you to stop and think before you react.

- Give each student a *Stop* sign. Then say:

    Put this sign in a spot where you can easily see it and be reminded of what to do when you are angry.

- Have the students put their *Triggers And Hot Buttons* activity sheet in their folders. Collect the folders.

TRIGGERS AND HOT BUTTONS

Directions: Complete the activity sheet below. When everyone has finished, you may share your thoughts with the group.

My *triggers* or *hot buttons* are:

Example:

When someone talks about my mom.

I can handle my anger by:

Example:

Using an *"I" Message*:

"When someone talks about my mom,
I feel angry, because my mom means a lot to me."

_____
_____
_____
_____
_____
_____
_____
_____
_____
_____

STOP!	So you can think before you act. Don't react!
THINK	What is the problem? What do I want? What can I do? What will happen if …? What is the best thing to do?
ACT	Carry out your plan.
CHECK	How did it work?

SESSION 6
ANGER-MANAGEMENT

Purpose:

To become aware of actions an angry person can take in order to "cool off"

Materials Required:

For the leader:
- ☐ *Group Opening* (page 9)
- ☐ *Group Rules* (page 10)
- ☐ Materials for *Energizer 6* (page 25)
- ☐ Chart paper
- ☐ Marker
- ☐ Chalkboard and chalk or dry-erase board and marker

Preparation:

Read the instructions for *Energizer 6*. Gather and prepare the necessary materials.

Write the following sentences on a piece of chart paper:

> I can handle this.
> He did that on purpose.
> He looked at me funny.
> I don't care what she thinks.
> He's talking about me.
> I am not losing control over that.
> It is not worth me getting upset over.
> She looked at me funny.

Session Content:

- Select a student to read the *Group Opening*.

- Pass the *Group Rules* around. Have each student read one rule aloud until all of the rules have been read.

- Present *Energizer 6*.

- Review the concept of *triggers* and *hot buttons*. Then say:

    Besides triggers *and* hot buttons, *there are* hot thoughts *and* cool thoughts. *A* hot thought *is one that may trigger your anger. A* cool thought *will help you stay calm. Look at the sentences written on the chart paper. Then decide whether you think each is a* hot thought *or a* cool thought.

- Create two columns on the board. Label one column *Hot Thoughts* and label the other column *Cool Thoughts*. Then say:

    Now that you understand what hot thoughts *and* cool thoughts *are, let's see if you can think of more. Go to the board and write your thoughts in the appropriate column.*

Give each student an opportunity to write his/her thoughts on the board. Review what is written in each column. Then ask:

Why is it better to think cool thoughts *than* hot thoughts*?*

Discuss the students' answers.

- Have the students stand in a straight line. Tell the first person in line to turn and face the second person in line. Then say:

    The first person in line should tell the second person one thing someone can do to "cool off," then walk to the back of the line. The person who was second in line and is now first turns and repeats the procedure. We will continue the activity until everyone has had a turn.

  Begin the activity. As students name ways to "cool off," write their suggestions on the board.

- Review what is written on the board. Then say:

    Our list could be much longer. What else can we add?

  Examples of ways to "cool off" may include:

    Imagine your favorite place
    Use positive self-talk
    Talk with someone
    Get out of the situation
    Use deep breathing
    Exercise
    Listen to music
    Write about what happened, then shred the paper

- Tell the students that many of the things a person can do to "cool off" are also healthy ways to handle anger.

SESSION 7
ANGER-MANAGEMENT

Purpose:

To discuss healthy ways to react to anger-provoking situations

Materials Required:

For the leader:
- ☐ *Group Opening* (page 9)
- ☐ *Group Rules* (page 10)
- ☐ Materials for *Energizer 7* (page 30)

For each student:
- ☐ Student's folder
- ☐ *Anger Thermometer* (page 62)
- ☐ Pencil

Preparation:

Read the instructions for *Energizer 7*. Gather and prepare the necessary materials.

Make a copy of *Anger Thermometer* for each student.

Session Content:

- Give each student his/her folder.

- Select a student to read the *Group Opening*.

- Pass the *Group Rules* around. Have each student read one rule aloud until all of the rules have been read.

- Present *Energizer 7*.

- Give each student a copy of *Anger Thermometer* and a pencil. Review the directions. Have the students complete the activity sheet.

- Using the completed *Anger Thermometer* activity sheet, discuss with the students what made them angry and where on the thermometer their anger fell. Then ask:

    What was the trigger?

    How did you react?

    From what you now know, what might be a better way to handle your anger?

- Give the students the following examples of triggers and have them tell where on the thermometer their anger would fall and how to handle the anger in a healthy way.

    1. Someone is gossiping about you behind your back.

    2. Someone takes your notebook with all your class notes.

    3. Your sister/brother wears your clothes without asking you.

    4. Your teacher says you did not turn in your homework. You know you did.

    Have the students give additional examples.

- Encourage the students to react in healthy ways when they are angry.

- Have the students put their activity sheets in their folders. Collect the folders.

ANGER THERMOMETER

Directions: Think of a time that you were angry this week. Beginning at 0, fill in the thermometer to the number that indicates how angry you felt.

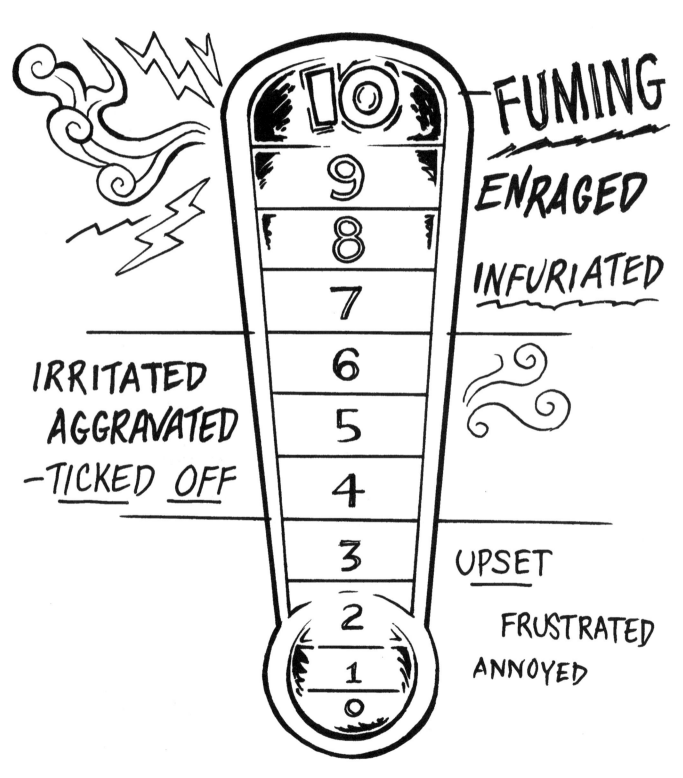

SESSION 8
ANGER-MANAGEMENT

Purpose:

To review the anger-management concepts presented during the past sessions

Materials Required:

For the leader:
- ☐ *Group Opening* (page 9)
- ☐ *Group Rules* (page 10)
- ☐ *Energizer 9* (page 31)
- ☐ *Bingo Numbers* (pages 42-43)
- ☐ Container

For each student:
- ☐ Student's folder
- ☐ *Anger Bingo* (page 65)
- ☐ Markers or pens of two different-color inks

Preparation:

Read the instructions for *Energizer 9*.

Make a copy of *Anger Bingo* for each student.

Make a copy of the *Bingo Numbers*. Cut the numbers apart and place them in the container.

Session Content:

- Give each student his/her folder.

- Select a student to read the *Group Opening*.

- Pass the *Group Rules* around. Have each student read one rule aloud until all of the rules have been read.

- Present *Energizer 9*.

- Tell the students:

  We are going to play Anger Bingo. *As we play this game, we will review things we have learned in the past few weeks.*

- Give each student a copy of *Anger Bingo* and markers or pens of two different-color inks. Explain how the students should fill in their bingo cards by saying:

  The letters A N G E R *are printed at the top of the columns. Below each letter is a number range. Using one color of ink/marker, fill in each circle in each column with one of the numbers within the indicated range. For example, you may choose 3, 5, 8, 12, and 15 to fill in the circles in the column under the letter* A.

- Explain how the game is played by saying:

  I will draw one number at a time from this container. As I draw each number, look at your Anger Bingo *card to see if you have written that number on your card. If you have that number on your card, raise your hand. I will call on you to complete the sentence written in that space. You may then place an X in the box using the other color of ink/marker. The first person to get five X's in a row should call out* Anger Bingo! *He or she will win the game.*

- Play the game.

- Discuss the statements on the *Anger Bingo* cards. Ask the students which were easy to complete and which were difficult.

- Have the students put their activity sheets in their folders. Collect the folders.

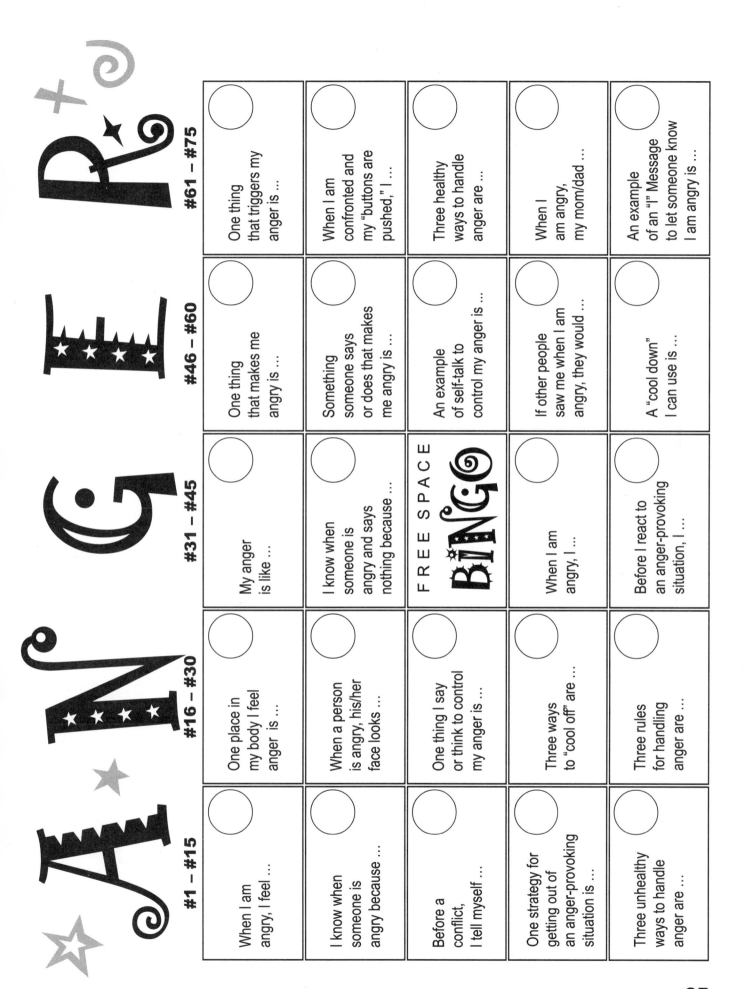

SESSION 9
ANGER-MANAGEMENT

Purpose:

To conclude the group

Materials Required:

For the leader:
- ☐ *Group Opening* (page 9)
- ☐ *Group Rules* (page 10)
- ☐ Materials for *Energizer 10* (page 32)

For each student:
- ☐ Student's folder
- ☐ Index cards
- ☐ Pencil

Preparation:

Read the instructions for *Energizer 10*. Gather the necessary materials.

Session Content:

- Give each student his/her folder and a pencil.

- Select a student to read the *Group Opening*.

- Pass the *Group Rules* around. Have each student read one rule aloud until all of the rules have been read.

- Present *Energizer 10*.

- Give each student, except the student to be featured, an index card. Give the following instructions to the group members who have been given index cards:

    1. *On your index card, write something nice about (NAME OF FEATURED STUDENT).*

    2. *You will each have a turn to be the featured student.*

    3. *Each of you will read your compliment aloud, then give your card to the student who is being featured.*

    Give each group member an opportunity to be the featured student. Then tell the students that if they ever feel low, they should take out the cards and read them. They may want to display them in their bedrooms at home and read them often.

- Review what the students have learned about anger and about how to handle it in a healthy way.

- Have the students go through their folders and give you any papers they want shredded. They may keep their folders and any papers they want.

- To conclude the group, have the students participate in the *Jelly Roll Squeeze* activity. Have the students stand side by side with their arms around each other's waists. Beginning on one end, tell the students to start to roll toward the other end. The first person should roll toward the second person, the second person should roll toward the third person, the third toward the fourth, on so on. When everyone is curled in, say, "Squeeze" on the count of three.

- Thank the students for participating in the group and for sharing with others.

BULLYING

SESSION 1
BULLYING

Purpose:

To introduce the group members to each other, explain the purpose of the group, and emphasize the importance of good listening skills

Materials Required:

For the leader:
- ☐ *Group Opening* (page 9)
- ☐ *Group Rules* (page 10)
- ☐ Materials for *Energizer 1* (page 13)
- ☐ Materials for *Energizer 2* (page 14)

For each student:
- ☐ 2-pocket manila folder
- ☐ Crayons or markers
- ☐ Pencil

Preparation:

If you have not already done so, reproduce the *Group Rules* and *Group Opening*. Laminate the pages if possible.

Read the instructions for *Energizer 1* and *Energizer 2*. Gather and prepare the necessary materials.

Session Content:

- Introduce the *Group Rules* and the *Group Opening* to the students.

- Present *Energizer 1*.

- Present *Energizer 2*.

- Give each student a folder, crayons or markers, and a pencil. Tell the students the folders will be used to hold their handouts.

- Instruct the students to write their name on the folder, along with the day and class period the group meets. Allow time for the students to use the crayons or markers to decorate their folders.

- Explain that the purpose of the group is to distinguish between *playful teasing* and *bullying* and to explore ways to deal with bullying.

- Collect the folders. (*Note:* The folders will be collected by the leader at the end of each session. At the final session, the students may keep whatever they want from their folders. Shred anything the students do not want to keep.)

SESSION 2
BULLYING

Purpose:

To define *bullying* and give input about bullying behaviors, causes, and places where bullying occurs

Materials Required:

For the leader:
- ☐ *Group Opening* (page 9)
- ☐ *Group Rules* (page 10)
- ☐ Materials for *Energizer 3* (page 22)
- ☐ Chart paper
- ☐ Markers
- ☐ Masking tape

Preparation:

Read the instructions for *Energizer 3*. Gather the necessary materials.

On one sheet of chart paper, write the following definition of *bullying*.

> *Bullying* is intentionally aggressive behavior. It is made up of repeated harmful acts that include an imbalance of power. Bullying is the most common form of violence. It is hurtful to the victim.

Label three sheets of chart paper:

1. *What do bullies do?*
2. *Why do kids get picked on?*
3. *Where does bullying take place?*

Attach the charts to the wall with masking tape.

Session Content:

- Select a student to read the *Group Opening*.

- Pass the *Group Rules* around. Have each student read one rule aloud until all of the rules have been read.

- Present *Energizer 3*.

- Show the students the chart paper with the definition of *bullying*. Review its meaning. Then say:

    There are three pieces of chart paper on the wall. There is a marker next to each piece of chart paper. Go to each piece of chart paper and write an answer for each question.

- Some things the students may write are:

    What do bullies do? *(Intimidate, name-call, fight, use insulting messages, demand money, damage or destroy property, etc.)*

    Why do kids get picked on? *(Appearance [clothes, hair, size], race, social status, etc. Bullying is usually about sensitive issues.)*

    Where does bullying take place? *(Gym, cafeteria, halls, restrooms, etc.)*

- After the students have finished writing, conclude the session by discussing their answers. Remove the wall charts and save the one with the definition of *bullying*.

SESSION 3
BULLYING

Purpose:

To identify physical and emotional bullying and emphasize what needs to be done if you witness or are the victim of a bullying act

Materials Required:

For the leader:
- ☐ *Group Opening* (page 9)
- ☐ *Group Rules* (page 10)
- ☐ Materials for *Energizer 4* (page 23)
- ☐ Chart paper
- ☐ Masking tape
- ☐ Chart with *bullying* definition from Session #2
- ☐ Chalkboard and chalk or dry-erase board and marker

For each student:
- ☐ Pad of sticky notes
- ☐ Pencil

Preparation:

Read the instructions for *Energizer 4*. Gather and prepare the necessary materials. Follow the directions for making the *Feelings Cube*.

Label two pieces of chart paper *Physical Bullying* and *Emotional Bullying*. Hang the chart with the *bullying* definition and the two new charts on the wall.

Session Content:

- Select a student to read the *Group Opening*.

- Pass the *Group Rules* around. Have each student read one rule aloud until all of the rules have been read.

- Present *Energizer 4*.

- Review the definition of *bullying* on the chart paper. Underline the words *repeated harmful acts, imbalance of power,* and *hurtful to the victim*.

- Give each student a pad of sticky notes and a pencil. Then say:

    Today, we are going to talk about physical bullying and emotional or psychological bullying. There are two charts on the wall. One chart has the words Physical Bullying *written at the top. The other chart has the words* Emotional Bullying *written at the top. Using your sticky notes, write all the ways you can think of that people bully physically. Write one way on each sticky note.*

- Have the students post the sticky notes on the *Physical Bullying* wall chart. Repeat the same exercise for *Emotional Bullying*.

- Review the ideas that the students wrote. Some examples may be:

    Physical—hitting, tripping, touching, etc.

    Emotional—ignoring, name-calling, intimidating, etc.

- Tell the students that:

    It is not another student's right to tell anyone that he or she is ugly, dumb, fat, skinny, or talk about whatever else he or she doesn't like about a person.

    It is important to stop emotional bullying before it becomes physical bullying.

    It is important to take power away from the bully.

    It is important to TELL when you are being bullied or when you see someone else being bullied.

- Conclude the session by asking:

    Why might someone not tell he or she is being bullied or has seen someone else being bullied?

- Write the students' responses on the board. Responses may include: The person is embarrassed, frightened, afraid of being called a *tattletale* or *snitch*, etc.

- Conclude the session by emphasizing the following ideas:

    Telling on a bully is NOT *tattling* or *snitching*. It is *reporting*.

    It takes a lot of courage to tell, but you MUST report bullying.

    You can ignore the bully, but don't ignore the bullying. Tell an adult about it.

SESSION 4
BULLYING

Purpose:

To help students recognize the difference between *bullying* and *teasing*

Materials Required:

For the leader:
- ☐ *Group Opening* (page 9)
- ☐ *Group Rules* (page 10)
- ☐ Materials for *Energizer 5* (page 24)

For each student:
- ☐ Student's folder
- ☐ *Bullying Or Teasing* (page 73)
- ☐ Pencil

Preparation:

Read the instructions for *Energizer 5*. Gather and prepare the necessary materials.

Make a copy of *Bullying Or Teasing* for each student.

Session Content:

- Give each student his/her folder.

- Select a student to read the *Group Opening*.

- Pass the *Group Rules* around. Have each student read one rule aloud until all of the rules have been read.

- Present *Energizer 5*.

- Tell the students:

   I often hear someone say, "I was just teasing," or "It was only a joke." If what is said or done is hurtful, it is not a joke. It is bullying. *Bullying doesn't stop, even if the person gets mad. If what we say or how we act is done in a friendly, laughing manner and is not hurtful, then it is* teasing. *I am going to give each of you a copy of the activity sheet titled* Bullying Or Teasing. *Complete it by writing examples of teasing and bullying. When everyone has finished, we will share our answers. Be sure you can give reasons why you think something is* teasing *or why you think it is* bullying.

- Give each student a copy of *Bullying Or Teasing* and a pencil. Tell the students how much time they have to complete the activity sheet.

- When the allotted time has elapsed, have the students justify their answers by explaining their reasons for each selection.

- Have the students put their activity sheets in their folders. Collect the folders.

BULLYING OR TEASING

Directions: In the boxes below, write examples of bullying and teasing. Be sure that you can justify your answers!

Bullying	Teasing

SESSION 5
BULLYING

Purpose:

To identify the persons involved in a bullying situation and the role each one plays

Materials Required:

For the leader:
- ☐ *Group Opening* (page 9)
- ☐ *Group Rules* (page 10)
- ☐ Materials for *Energizer 6* (page 25)

For each student:
- ☐ Student's folder
- ☐ *The Roles In Bullying Situations* (page 75)
- ☐ Pencil

Preparation:

Read the instructions for *Energizer 6*. Gather and prepare the necessary materials.

Make a copy of *The Roles In Bullying Situations* for each student.

Session Content:

- Give each student his/her folder.

- Select a student to read the *Group Opening*.

- Pass the *Group Rules* around. Have each student read one rule aloud until all of the rules have been read.

- Present *Energizer 6*.

- Review the differences between *bullying* and *teasing* from the last session. Then say:

    Today, we are going to recognize the roles people play in bullying situations.

- Give each student a copy of *The Roles In Bullying Situations* and a pencil. Review the directions. Tell the students how much time they have to complete the activity sheet.

- When the allotted time has elapsed, review the students' answers. Have those students who wish to do so tell about a time when they were in one of the roles listed on the activity sheet. The answers to the activity sheet are: 5; 6; 1; 2; 4; 3.

- Have the students put their activity sheets in their folders. Collect the folders.

THE ROLES IN BULLYING SITUATIONS

Directions: Match the person(s) to the role he/she plays in bullying situations. Put the number of the role on the line next to the description of the role.

1. Victim   _____ stay away, don't take sides

2. Ringleader Bully   _____ step in and/or stick up for the victim

3. Assistant Bullies   _____ person who is the target of the bully

4. Reinforcers   _____ person who plays the main role in bullying

5. Outsiders   _____ persons who laugh with or encourage the bully

6. Defenders   _____ persons who join in the bullying

Write about a time when you found yourself in one of these roles. Tell what your role was and describe the situation.

_____

_____

_____

_____

_____

_____

_____

SESSION 6
BULLYING

Purpose:

To examine behaviors exhibited during a bullying situation and help students become aware of some strategies to defuse bullying

Materials Required:

For the leader:
- ☐ *Group Opening* (page 9)
- ☐ *Group Rules* (page 10)
- ☐ Materials for *Energizer 7* (page 30)
- ☐ Chart paper
- ☐ Marker
- ☐ Masking Tape

For each student:
- ☐ Student's folder
- ☐ Pad of sticky notes
- ☐ Pencil
- ☐ *Bullying Strategies* (page 78)

Preparation:

Read the instructions for *Energizer 7*. Gather and prepare the necessary materials.

Label four sheets of chart paper:

Strategies To Stop Bullying
Reasons Why People Won't Intervene
What I Can Do If Am Being Bullied
Girls/Boys

Attach the charts to the wall with masking tape.

Make a copy of *Bullying Strategies* for each student.

Session Content:

- Give each student his/her folder.

- Select a student to read the *Group Opening*.

- Pass the *Group Rules* around. Have each student read one rule aloud until all of the rules have been read.

- Present *Energizer 7*.

- Give each student a pad of sticky notes and a pencil. Then say:

    You see someone being bullied and you want to defend the victim. What can you do? Write down on the sticky notes any strategies you can think of that would help you defend the victim. Write only one strategy on each sticky note. When you have finished, put the sticky notes on the Strategies To Stop Bullying *chart.*

- Read what the students wrote and discuss each idea and its potential effectiveness. Some examples may be:

    Intervene and say something

    Get help

    Comfort the victim

- Continue the session by saying:

    This time, think about why someone might choose to be an outsider and do nothing when he or she sees someone being bullied. Write your answers on your sticky notes, then put the notes on the Reasons Why People Won't Intervene *chart.*

- Read what the students wrote and discuss each idea and its potential effectiveness. Some examples may be:

    Afraid the bully will turn on them

    Don't want to get involved

- Continue the session by saying:

    Now, put yourself in the position of the victim. Write on the sticky notes what you can do to help yourself if you are being bullied. When you have finished, put the sticky notes on the What I Can Do If I Am Being Bullied *chart.*

- Read what the students wrote and discuss each idea and its potential effectiveness. Some examples may be:

    Walk away

    Yell, "Stop!"

    Leave and get an adult

- Give each student a copy of *Bullying Strategies*. Review the strategies with the students. Have the students practice standing tall, with their shoulders back, and staring without talking. Then say:

    What you have just done is one effective technique a group can use to stop bullying.

- Have the students brainstorm about the similarities and differences in the ways boys and girls bully. Write the students' ideas on a piece of chart paper. After each idea, write a *B* if the students think it is a way boys bully and write a *G* if the students think it is a way girls bully. If both boys and girls would bully in the suggested manner, write both letters. The students will notice that girls' bullying usually involves social relationships. Girls more often than boys will bully with gossip, isolation, silent treatment, exclusion, or other indirect types of bullying. Historically, boys have exhibited more physically aggressive and direct behavior when they bully. But in recent years, girls have become more aggressive. Girls tend to bully girls, while boys will bully girls and other boys.

- Have the students put their activity sheets in their folders. Collect the folders.

BULLYING STRATEGIES

 It is very important to report bullying to an adult.

You can ignore the bully,
but do not ignore the bullying—
tell someone.

Don't be a ring leader,
assistant bully, reinforcer, or outsider.

Be a defender!
Step in and help.

If as a group you are witnessing bullying,
you can stand tall, shoulders back,
and stare at the bully while
someone goes to get an adult for help.

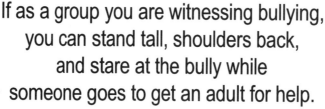

Always tell an adult if
you have been bullied
or are a witness to bullying.

SESSION 7
BULLYING

Purpose:

To review the bullying concepts presented during the past sessions

Materials Required:

For the leader:
- ☐ *Group Opening* (page 9)
- ☐ *Group Rules* (page 10)
- ☐ Materials for *Energizer 8* (page 31)
- ☐ *Bingo Numbers* (pages 42-43)
- ☐ Container

For each student:
- ☐ Student's folder
- ☐ *Bully Bingo* (page 81)
- ☐ Markers or pens of two different-color inks

Preparation:

Read the instructions for *Energizer 8*. Gather the necessary materials.

Make a copy of *Bully Bingo* for each student.

Make a copy of the *Bingo Numbers*. Cut the numbers apart and place them in the container.

Session Content:

- Give each student his/her folder.

- Select a student to read the *Group Opening*.

- Pass the *Group Rules* around. Have each student read one rule aloud until all of the rules have been read.

- Present *Energizer 8*.

- Tell the students:

    This is our last session, and I want to thank you for being in the group. Before we end this session, we are going to play Bully Bingo. *As we play this game, we will review things we have learned in the past few weeks.*

- Give each student a copy of *Bully Bingo* and markers or pens of two different-color inks. Explain how the students should fill in their bingo cards by saying:

    The letters B U L L Y *are printed at the top of the columns. Below each letter is a number range. Using one color of ink/marker, fill in each circle in each column with one of the numbers within the indicated range. For example, you may choose 3, 5, 8, 12, and 15 to fill in the circles in the column under the letter* B.

- Explain how the game is played by saying:

    I will draw one number at a time from this container. As I draw each number, look at your Bully Bingo *card to see if you have written that number on your card. If you have that number on your card, raise your hand. I will call on you to answer the question written in that space. You may then place an X in the box using the other color of ink/marker. The first person to get five X's in a row should call out* Bully Bingo! *He or she will win the game.*

- Play the game.

- Discuss the statements on the *Bully Bingo* cards. Ask the students which were easy to complete and which were difficult.

- Have the students go through their folders and give you any papers they want shredded. They may keep their folders and any papers they want.

- To conclude the group, have the students participate in the *Jelly Roll Squeeze* activity. Have the students stand side by side with their arms around each other's waists. Beginning on one end, tell the students to start to roll toward the other end. The first person should roll toward the second person, the second person should roll toward the third person, the third toward the fourth, on so on. When everyone is curled in, say, "Squeeze" on the count of three.

- Thank the students for participating in the group and for sharing with others.

BINGO

	B #1 – #15	O #16 – #30	I #31 – #45	L #46 – #60	Y #61 – #75
	What is the most important thing to do if you see someone being bullied?	Name one reason someone might be a bully.	Tell about a time you were bullied.	Name two places bullying takes place.	What is the most important thing to do if you are being bullied?
	Describe one way girls bully and one way boys bully.	What is the difference between *bullying* and *teasing*?	Define *bullying*.	Give two examples of bullying.	Who is the *ringleader bully*?
	Who is the victim?	Tell about a time you saw someone being bullied.	FREE SPACE BINGO	What does the *outsider* do?	Name two things you can do to help a victim.
	What role do reinforcers play?	Give two examples of *emotional bullying*.	Who can you tell if you are being bullied?	Describe something a bully might do.	What can a group of students do to stand up to a bully?
	Give two examples of *physical bullying*.	What role do *defenders* play?	Why would someone not tell about bullying?	Who can you tell if you see someone being bullied?	What do *assistant bullies* do?

GRAB BAG GUIDANCE © 2005 MAR★CO PRODUCTS, INC. 1-800-448-2197

81

COPING SKILLS

SESSION 1
COPING SKILLS

Purpose:

To introduce the group members to each other, explain the purpose of the group, and emphasize the importance of good listening skills

Materials Required:

For the leader:
- ☐ *Group Opening* (page 9)
- ☐ *Group Rules* (page 10)
- ☐ Materials for *Energizer 1* (page 13)
- ☐ Materials for *Energizer 2* (page 14)

For each student:
- ☐ 2-pocket manila folder
- ☐ Crayons or markers
- ☐ Pencil

Preparation:

If you have not already done so, reproduce the *Group Rules* and *Group Opening*. Laminate the pages if possible.

Read the instructions for *Energizer 1* and *Energizer 2*. Gather and prepare the necessary materials.

Session Content:

- Introduce the *Group Rules* and the *Group Opening* to the students.

- Present *Energizer 1*.

- Give each student a folder, crayons or markers, and a pencil. Tell the students the folders will be used to hold their handouts.

- Instruct the students to write their names on the folder, along with the day and class period the group meets. Allow time for the students to use the crayons or markers to decorate their folders.

- Explain to the students that the purpose of the group is to explore ways to cope with problems or difficulties. The group's goal is for students to apply the skills they will learn in this group to their real-life situations.

- Present *Energizer 2* to reinforce the concept that listening to each other while participating in the sessions is very important.

- Collect the folders. (*Note:* The folders will be collected by the leader at the end of each session. At the final session, the students may keep whatever they want from their folders. Shred anything the students do not want to keep.)

SESSION 2
COPING SKILLS

Purpose:

To explore ways of coping

Materials Required:

For the leader:
- ☐ *Group Opening* (page 9)
- ☐ *Group Rules* (page 10)
- ☐ Materials for *Energizer 3* (page 22)
- ☐ Chalkboard and chalk or dry-erase board and marker

For each student:
- ☐ Student's folder
- ☐ Package of sticky notes
- ☐ Pencil
- ☐ *Formula To Help You Cope* (page 87)

Preparation:

Read the instructions for *Energizer 3*. Gather the necessary materials.

Make a copy of *Formula To Help You Cope* for each student.

Session Content:

- Give each student his/her folder.

- Select a student to read the *Group Opening*.

- Pass the *Group Rules* around. Have each student read one rule aloud until all of the rules have been read.

- Present *Energizer 3*.

- Tell the students:

  Feeling pain is a signal to your brain that you need help or need to do something to get rid of the pain. When it comes to situations that cause emotional pain, you must learn to cope. Of course, one way to cope is to reach out and get help. But there are other ways to cope. During our group sessions, we will learn some of these coping skills.

- Have the students brainstorm a list of situations over which people have no control. Write these on the board. Some examples could be:

  Divorce
  Death
  Alcoholic parent

- Emphasize that people need to accept things they cannot change. Stress that there are some painful situations, such as abuse or violent behavior, that no one should accept. In situations like these, we must look to others for help. We cannot handle these situations by ourselves.

- Write the words *Coping Skills* on the board. Give each student sticky notes and a pencil. Tell the students to write all the ways they can think of that people cope. Have them stick the notes on the board. Review each suggestion.

- Tell the students:

    When coping, it is very important not to hurt yourself, hurt others, or damage or destroy property. Look at the coping suggestions on the board. Go to the board and remove any sticky notes that refer to things that are hurtful.

- Read the remaining sticky notes, which suggest healthy ways to cope with problems or difficulties.

- Give each student a copy of *Formula To Help You Cope*. Review the activity sheet with the students. Discuss the meaning of each suggestion.

- Tell the students that upcoming sessions will explore a formula to help them cope.

- Have the students put their activity sheets in their folders. Collect the folders.

SESSION 3
COPING SKILLS

Purpose:

To examine the ways students care for themselves and others and the ways others care for them

Materials Required:

For the leader:
- ☐ *Group Opening* (page 9)
- ☐ *Group Rules* (page 10)
- ☐ Materials for *Energizer 4* (page 23)
- ☐ Chalkboard and chalk or dry-erase board and marker

For each student:
- ☐ Student's folder
- ☐ *Me* (page 89)
- ☐ *Others* (page 90)
- ☐ Pencil

Preparation:

Read the instructions for *Energizer 4*. Gather and prepare the necessary materials.

Make a copy of *Me* and *Others* for each student.

Session Content:

- Give each student his/her folder.

- Select a student to read the *Group Opening*.

- Pass the *Group Rules* around. Have each student read one rule aloud until all of the rules have been read.

- Present *Energizer 4*.

- Say to the students:

    In the last session, we learned the Formula To Help You Cope. *What did the C in the formula stand for?* (Care for yourself and others.) *Today's activity will focus on that idea.*

- Give each student a copy of *Me* and a pencil. Have the students think of ways they care for themselves physically, emotionally, and mentally and write them on the lines. Then have the students complete the sentence at the bottom of the page. Have the students share their answers with the group.

- Give each student a copy of *Others*. Have the students write on the lines what they do for others. Then say:

    *It is important to not only care for yourself, but also to care for others. Caring for others raises your self-esteem. That, in turn, improves your emotional well-being. Complete the sentence at the bottom of the page by describing one thing you **will** do for another person.*

- Have the students share the ways in which they care for other people. List all of these ways on the board. Discuss the list.

- Have the students put their activity sheets in their folders. Collect the folders.

Directions: On the lines below, write the ways that you can care for yourself physically, emotionally, and mentally. If you need more lines, you may add them.

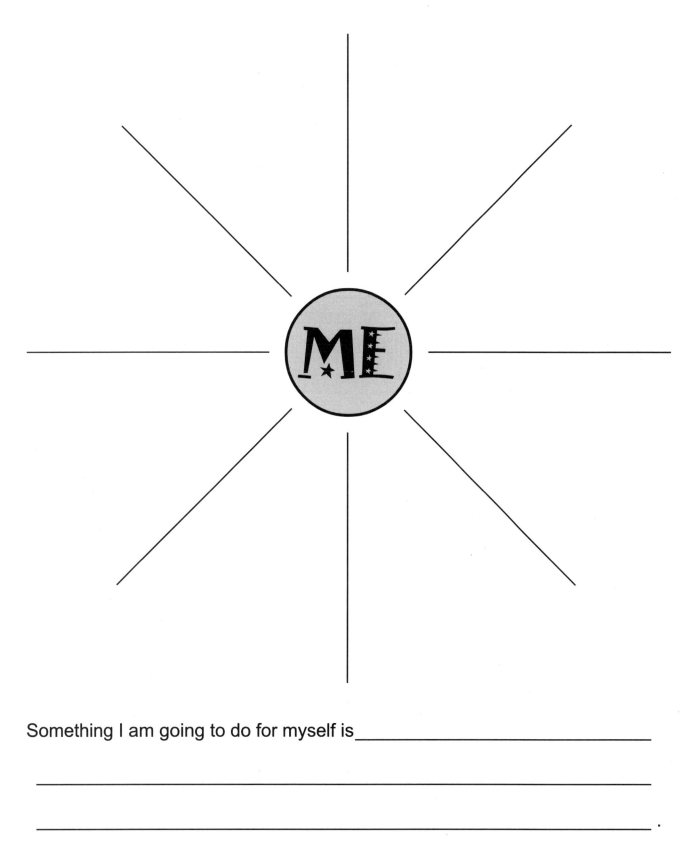

Something I am going to do for myself is _____

_____

_____ .

Directions: On the lines below, write the ways that you care or have cared for others. If you need more lines, you may add them.

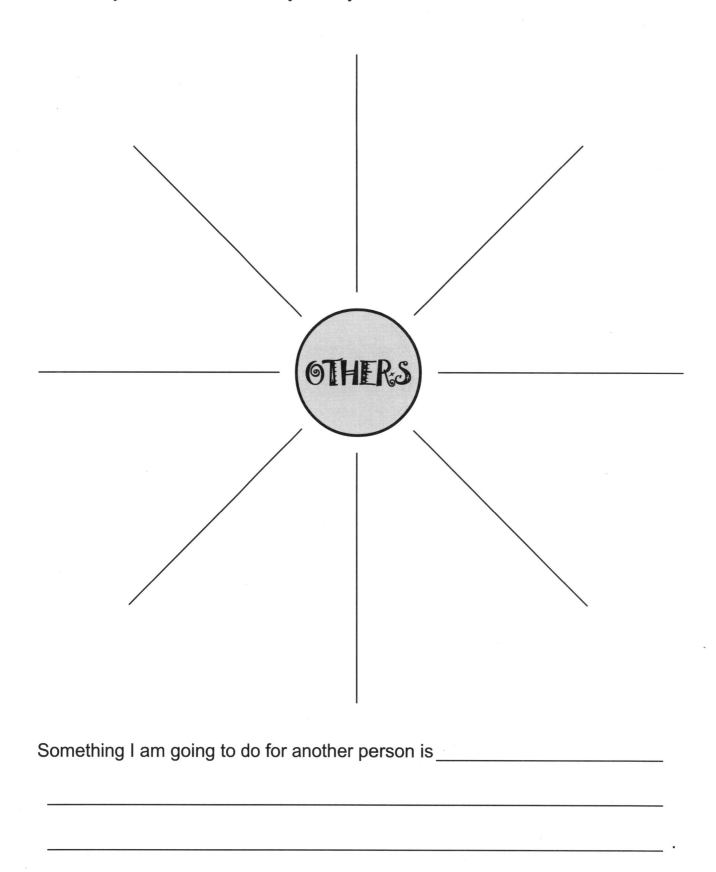

Something I am going to do for another person is _____

_____

_____.

SESSION 4
COPING SKILLS

Purpose:

To help students understand the components of an "I" Message and the difference between and "I" Message and a blaming message

Materials Required:

For the leader:
- ☐ *Group Opening* (page 9)
- ☐ *Group Rules* (page 10)
- ☐ Materials for *Energizer 5* (page 24)
- ☐ Chalkboard and chalk or dry-erase board and marker

For each student:
- ☐ Student's folder
- ☐ Pencil

For each pair of students:
- ☐ *"I" Message/Blaming Message* (page 93)

Preparation:

Read the instructions for *Energizer 5*. Gather and prepare the necessary materials.

Make a copy of *"I" Message/Blaming Message* for each pair of students.

Session Content:

- Give each student his/her folder.

- Select a student to read the *Group Opening*.

- Pass the *Group Rules* around. Have each student read one rule aloud until all of the rules have been read.

- Present *Energizer 5*.

- Tell the students:

  In the COPE formula, the O stands for Open Up And Communicate. *It is important to let people know how you feel, and/or what you think, by communicating with them.*

  A simple "I" Message is a good way to communicate how you feel about something. By using an "I" Message, you can let someone know how you feel without blaming him or her. When we tell another person how we feel, it often sounds like we are blaming the other person. The other person then becomes defensive and problems may arise.

- Write the following on the board:

  "I" Messages have three components:

  1. How you feel
  2. The behavior
  3. How the behavior affects you

  I feel _____ ,
  when _____
  because _____ .

- Give an example of an *"I" Message* by saying:

  *An example of an "I" Message is: I feel **mad**, when **someone takes my pencils** because **I need them to complete my work**.*

  "I" Messages don't have to be stated in this order. As long as the statement has the three components, the order doesn't matter.

  *Another example of an "I" Message in a different order is: When **someone takes my pencils**, I feel **angry** because **I can't complete my work**.*

  A blaming message would sound like: You took my pencils. Or: I am mad because you took my pencils.

- Ask the students:

  Can you tell the difference between the "I" Message and the blaming message? (The "I" Message states how you feel.)

  Let the students know that it is important for them to state why they feel the way they do when using "I" Messages because no one can argue with them about how they feel.

  It is also important that students know "I" Messages can be used to communicate in a positive way such as: *I feel happy when people remember my birthday.*

- Divide the students into pairs. Give each pair of students a copy of *"I" Message/Blaming Message* and two pencils. Have the students complete the activity sheet, then share their answers with the group.

- Have the students explain the difference between an "I" Message and a blaming message. Discuss why an "I" Message is more effective.

- Have the students decide which member of each pair will put the activity sheet in his/her folder. Collect the folders.

"I" MESSAGE/BLAMING MESSAGE

Directions: Write one "I" Message and one blaming message for each of the following scenarios.

Your parents are divorced and your dad talks badly about your mom. Let your dad know how you feel about this.

"I" Message _____
_____
_____.

Blaming Message _____
_____
_____.

Your brother took your DVD without asking.

"I" Message _____
_____
_____.

Blaming Message _____
_____
_____.

Your mom told you she would take you to the mall, but now she is too tired to go.

"I" Message _____
_____
_____.

Blaming Message _____
_____
_____.

Your friend told your secret to another friend.

"I" Message _____
_____
_____.

Blaming Message _____
_____
_____.

SESSION 5
COPING SKILLS

Purpose:

To make students aware of the three types of communication—assertive, non-assertive, and aggressive

Materials Required:

For the leader:
- ☐ *Group Opening* (page 9)
- ☐ *Group Rules* (page 10)
- ☐ Materials for *Energizer 7* (page 30)
- ☐ Chart paper
- ☐ Marker
- ☐ Masking tape
- ☐ *Communication Role-Plays* (page 96)
- ☐ Scissors

For each student:
- ☐ 9 Sticky notes

Preparation:

Read the instructions for *Energizer 7*. Gather and prepare the necessary materials.

Title three pieces of chart paper: *Eye Contact, Body Language,* and *Tone Of Voice*. Divide each chart into three columns labeled *Assertive, Non-Assertive,* and *Aggressive*. Hang the charts in the room.

Make a copy of *Communication Role-Plays*. Cut the role-play descriptions into strips.

Session Content:

- Select a student to read the *Group Opening*.

- Pass the *Group Rules* around. Have each student read one rule aloud until all of the rules have been read.

- Present *Energizer 7*.

- Review "I" Messages with the students. Discuss why using "I" Messages is an effective way to communicate. Then say:

    Today, we are going to talk more about communication. The way a person communicates is important. There are three types of communication:

    Assertive communication lets people know how you feel in a non-threatening way.

    Non-assertive communication is not an effective way to communicate, because you don't clearly state what you want.

    Aggressive communication is a threatening way to communicate.

- Begin with the *Eye Contact* chart. Give each student three sticky notes. Have the students write or draw on the sticky notes how an assertive, non-assertive, and aggressive person would make eye contact.

Then have them put their sticky notes in the correct area of the chart. Review what the students wrote or drew.

Answers may include:

Assertive—look directly at the person

Non-Assertive—little or no eye contact

Aggressive—squinting, scowling

- Go to the *Body Language* chart. Give each student three sticky notes. Have the students write or draw on the sticky notes how an assertive, non-assertive, and aggressive person's body language might look. Then have them put their sticky notes in the correct area of the chart. Review what the students wrote or drew.

Answers may include:

Assertive—straight, standing tall, shoulders facing other person

Non-Assertive—hunched over, body turned away from the other person

Aggressive—leaning toward the other person in a threatening way, crowding into his/her "space"

- Then go to the chart titled *Tone Of Voice*. Give each student three sticky notes. Have the students write or draw on the sticky notes how an assertive, non-assertive, and aggressive person's voice might sound. Then have them put their sticky notes in the correct area of the chart. Review what the students wrote or drew.

Answers may include:

Assertive—calm, clear voice; speaking directly to the other person

Non-Assertive—quiet, questioning instead of stating

Aggressive—loud, gruff

- Divide the group members into pairs. Give each pair a situation to role-play. One partner will read the description of the situation. The other partner will act it out, using the specified communication technique. Remind the students to use the appropriate eye contact, body language, and tone of voice. After each role-play, the other group members will guess if the student showed assertive, non-assertive, or aggressive communication.

- Conclude the session by having the students explain why assertive communication is the most effective.

COMMUNICATION ROLE-PLAYS

Directions: Cut the role-play descriptions into strips. Give one strip to each pair of students.

ASSERTIVE

STUDENT #1 READS THE DESCRIPTION OF THE SITUATION:
Mary doesn't want to partner with Sue for the science project.

STUDENT #2 ACTS OUT THE SITUATION, SAYING:
Let's not be partners for this project.

NON-ASSERTIVE

STUDENT #1 READS THE DESCRIPTION OF THE SITUATION:
Tom took Megan's pencil.

STUDENT #2 ACTS OUT THE SITUATION, SAYING:
I would like my pencil back, please.

AGGRESSIVE

STUDENT #1 READS THE DESCRIPTION OF THE SITUATION:
Joe doesn't want to sit with Steve at lunch today.

STUDENT #2 ACTS OUT THE SITUATION, SAYING:
I want to sit with someone else at the lunch table.

ASSERTIVE

STUDENT #1 READS THE DESCRIPTION OF THE SITUATION:
Kris asks the teacher if she may work alone on a project.

STUDENT #2 ACTS OUT THE SITUATION, SAYING:
I really don't like to work in groups. May I work alone?

NON-ASSERTIVE

STUDENT #1 READS THE DESCRIPTION OF THE SITUATION:
Julie needs a ride home from the student council meeting.

STUDENT #2 ACTS OUT THE SITUATION, SAYING:
Do you think your mom could give me a ride home from the meeting?

SESSION 6
COPING SKILLS

Purpose:

To teach students to change negative thoughts into positive thoughts

Materials Required:

For the leader:
- ☐ *Group Opening* (page 9)
- ☐ *Group Rules* (page 10)
- ☐ *Energizer 11* (page 32)
- ☐ Chalkboard and chalk or dry-erase board and marker

For each student:
- ☐ Student's folder
- ☐ *Negative Thoughts ⇨ Positive Thoughts* (page 99)
- ☐ *Ways To Raise Self-Esteem* (page 100)
- ☐ Pencil

Preparation:

Read the instructions for *Energizer 11*.

Make a copy of *Negative Thoughts ⇨ Positive Thoughts* and *Ways To Raise Self-Esteem* for each student.

Session Content:

- Give each student his/her folder.

- Select a student to read the *Group Opening*.

- Pass the *Group Rules* around. Have each student read one rule aloud until all of the rules have been read.

- Present *Energizer 11*.

- Ask the students:

    What does the P in the COPE formula stand for? (The P stands for positive thinking.) *Today's lesson will focus on positive thinking.*

    The Chinese character for crisis is composed of elements that signify danger and opportunity. Can you tell what you think this means?

    People must deal with painful situations in their lives. One way to cope with a painful situation is to try to make something positive result from the situation. It is like the saying,

GRAB BAG GUIDANCE © 2005 MAR*CO PRODUCTS, INC. 1-800-448-2197

"When life gives you lemons, make lemonade."

One way you can achieve this is through positive thinking. You have the power and control over what you tell yourself. Turning negative thoughts into positive thoughts will not only raise your self-esteem, it will also help you cope.

- Ask the students to name negative thoughts. Write their ideas on the board.

- Give each student a copy of *Negative Thoughts ⇨ Positive Thoughts* and a pencil. Tell the students to select five negative thoughts from the list on the board, turn them into positive thoughts, and write positive thoughts on their activity sheet. Have the students share their results.

- Give each student a copy of *Ways To Raise Self-Esteem*. Have the students take turns reading the suggestions and discuss each one as it is read. Then have the students add some of their own suggestions.

- Have the students put their activity sheets in their folders. Collect the folders.

NEGATIVE THOUGHTS ⇨ POSITIVE THOUGHTS

1. NEGATIVE ⇨ ⇨ ⇨ ⇨ ⇨ ⇨ ⇨ 1. POSITIVE ☆

_____   _____
_____   _____
_____   _____

2. NEGATIVE ⇨ ⇨ ⇨ ⇨ ⇨ ⇨ ⇨ 2. POSITIVE ☆

_____   _____
_____   _____
_____   _____

3. NEGATIVE ⇨ ⇨ ⇨ ⇨ ⇨ ⇨ ⇨ 3. POSITIVE ☆

_____   _____
_____   _____
_____   _____

4. NEGATIVE ⇨ ⇨ ⇨ ⇨ ⇨ ⇨ ⇨ 4. POSITIVE ☆

_____   _____
_____   _____
_____   _____

5. NEGATIVE ⇨ ⇨ ⇨ ⇨ ⇨ ⇨ ⇨ 5. POSITIVE ☆

_____   _____
_____   _____
_____   _____

You have the power to control your thoughts.
Thinking positively enhances your self-esteem and makes you feel better.

WAYS TO RAISE SELF-ESTEEM

- Accept yourself. Be satisfied with who you are.

- Do things for others. You will find that helping others makes you feel good. The way you treat others is the way they will treat you.

- Give yourself a break. Don't be so tough on yourself. Sometimes people are so hard on themselves that they are their own worst enemies. You are human. You are going to make mistakes, and you will learn from them.

- Enjoy yourself and the world around you.

- Act like people whom you respect.

- Focus on the positive, not the negative.

- Don't be afraid to take risks. It is okay to fail.

- Don't compare yourself to other people.

- S + R = O. This means: **Situation** + how you **react** or **respond** = **outcome**. If you don't like what is happening to you (outcome), then change the way you respond to things.

- Let go of past regrets. You must let go of the past in order to move ahead.

SESSION 7
COPING SKILLS

Purpose:

To encourage the students to examine their feelings in relation to situations they have experienced

Materials Required:

For the leader:
- ☐ *Group Opening* (page 9)
- ☐ *Group Rules* (page 10)
- ☐ Materials for *Energizer 6* (page 25)
- ☐ Chalkboard and chalk or dry-erase board and marker

For each student:
- ☐ Student's folder
- ☐ *Feelings Sentence Completion* (page 102)
- ☐ Pencil

Preparation:

Read the instructions for *Energizer 6*. Gather and prepare the necessary materials.

Make a copy of *Feelings Sentence Completion* for each student.

Session Content:

- Give each student his/her folder.

- Select a student to read the *Group Opening*.

- Pass the *Group Rules* around. Have each student read one rule aloud until all of the rules have been read.

- Present *Energizer 6*.

- Ask the students:

    What does the letter E *stand for in the COPE formula?* (It stands for expressing your emotions or feelings.) *It is important to identify and express the emotions you are feeling. You need to recognize how you feel and realize there are no good or bad feelings. All feelings are acceptable.*

    What is important is how you handle your feelings. Remember: It is not okay to hurt yourself, hurt others, or damage or destroy property.

- Ask the students to name as many feelings or emotions as they can. As each feeling or emotion is mentioned, write the word on the board. Then add your own suggestions to the list. Review the list with the students.

- Give each student a copy of *Feelings Sentence Completion* and a pencil. Have the students share their completed activity sheets with the group.

- Ask the students to look at their *Feelings Sentence Completion* activity sheet and select one statement. Have each student describe how he/she would have felt differently if the situation that caused the feeling were changed.

- Have the students put their activity sheets in their folders. Collect the folders.

FEELINGS SENTENCE COMPLETION

Directions: Fill in the blanks to complete each sentence.

1. A time I felt happy was _____
   _____ .

2. A time I felt sad was _____
   _____ .

3. A time I felt confused was _____
   _____ .

4. A time I felt accepted was _____
   _____ .

5. A time I felt furious was _____
   _____ .

6. A time I felt lonely was _____
   _____ .

7. I time I felt surprised was _____
   _____ .

8. A time I felt ecstatic was _____
   _____ .

9. A time I felt content was _____
   _____ .

10. A time I felt anxious was _____
    _____ .

SESSION 8
COPING SKILLS

Purpose:

To help the students realize they can bounce back from adversity and identify people who can support them in this endeavor

Materials Required:

For the leader:
- ☐ *Group Opening* (page 9)
- ☐ *Group Rules* (page 10)
- ☐ *Energizer 9* (page 31)
- ☐ Chalkboard and chalk or dry-erase board and marker
- ☐ Rubber ball

For each student:
- ☐ Student's folder
- ☐ *People Who Support Me* (page 105)
- ☐ Pencil

Preparation:

Read the instructions for *Energizer 9*.

Make a copy of *People Who Support Me* for each student.

Session Content:

- Give each student his/her folder.

- Select a student to read the *Group Opening*.

- Pass the *Group Rules* around. Have each student read one rule aloud until all of the rules have been read.

- Present *Energizer 9*.

- Review the formula for coping:

    C care for yourself and others
    O open up and communicate
    P positive thinking
    E express emotions

- Introduce the word *resiliency* by explaining that it means *the ability to bounce back*. Bounce a rubber ball to show how it comes back up after being tossed down. Then say:

    Everyone has the ability to bounce back from a difficult or painful situation. Can you name some situations that you believe are difficult or painful? (Answers may include illness, depression, loss, etc.)

- Record the students' answers on the board. Then continue the session by saying:

    You may have read about people who have had to deal with adversities and have bounced back. Helen Keller, who lost her sight and hearing while still a baby and didn't learn to speak until she was nearly 10 years old, rose above her disabilities. Heather Mills McCartney, singer Paul McCartney's wife, lost a leg when hit by a motorcycle. Can you think of any other people who have risen above adversities?

As the students answer the question, write on the board the names they mention.

- Discuss the people the students selected and the ways in which those people were able to rise above adversities. Then say:

  Everyone has the ability to rise above adversities. What do you think can help you be resilient? (Write the students' answers on the board.)

- When the list is complete, note that some or all of the students' suggestions may include the steps in the *COPE* formula and may include the support of family and friends.

- Give each student a copy of *People Who Support Me* and a pencil. Tell the students to complete the activity sheet. Then ask the students to share with the group the names of people they chose to support them. You may identify additional family, friends, teachers, coaches, etc. who can help them become resilient.

- Have the students put their activity sheets in their folders. Collect the folders.

PEOPLE WHO SUPPORT ME

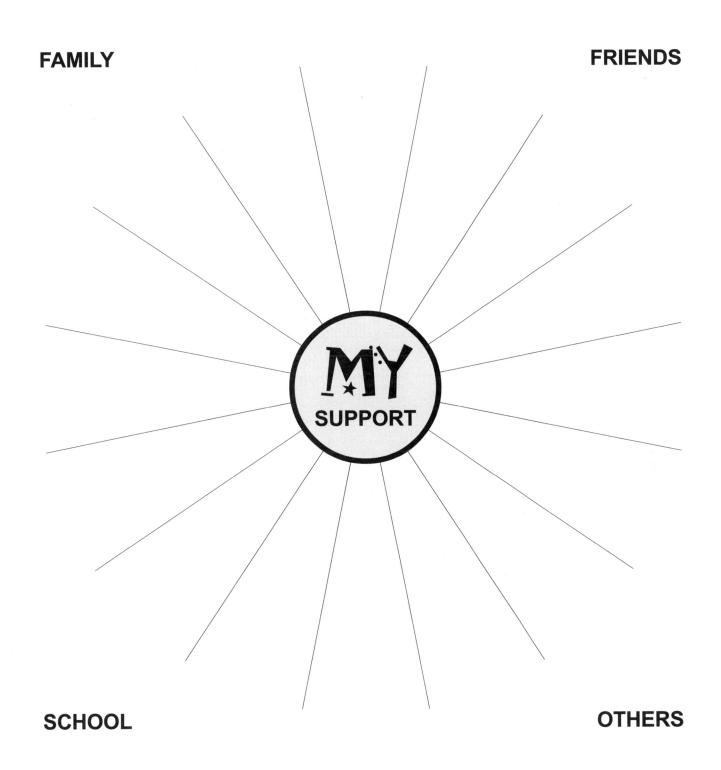

SESSION 9
COPING SKILLS

Purpose:

To review the concepts that have been presented in previous lessons

Materials Required:

For the leader:
- ☐ *Group Opening* (page 9)
- ☐ *Group Rules* (page 10)
- ☐ Materials for *Energizer 10* (page 32)
- ☐ *Bingo Numbers* (pages 42-43)
- ☐ Container

For each student:
- ☐ Student's folder
- ☐ *Cope Bingo* (page 108)
- ☐ Markers or pens of two different-color inks

Preparation:

Read the instructions for *Energizer 10*. Gather the necessary materials.

Make a copy of *Cope Bingo* for each student.

Make a copy of the *Bingo Numbers*. Cut the numbers apart and place them in the container.

Session Content:

- Give each student his/her folder.

- Select a student to read the *Group Opening*.

- Pass the *Group Rules* around. Have each student read one rule aloud until all of the rules have been read.

- Present *Energizer 10*.

- Tell the students:

    This is our last session, and I want to thank you for being in the group. Before we end this session, we are going to play Cope Bingo. *As we play this game, we will review things we have learned in the past few weeks.*

- Give each student a copy of *Cope Bingo* and markers or pens of two different-color inks. Explain how the students should fill in their bingo cards by saying:

    The letters C O P E and a smiley face (☺) are printed at the top of the columns. Below each letter is a number range. Using one color of ink/marker, fill in each circle in each column with one of the numbers within the indicated range. For example, you may choose 3, 5, 8, 12, and 15 to fill in the circles in the column under the letter C.

- Explain how the game is played by saying:

    I will draw one number at a time from this container. As I draw each number, look at your Cope Bingo *card to see if you have written that number on your card. If you have that number on your card, raise your hand. I will call on you to answer the question written in that space. You may then place an X in the box using the other color of ink/marker. The first person to get five X's in a row should call out* Cope Bingo! *He or she will win the game.*

- Play the game.

- Discuss the statements on the *Cope Bingo* cards. Ask the students which were easy to complete and which were difficult.

- Have the students go through their folders and give you any papers they want shredded. They may keep their folders and any papers they want.

- To conclude the group, have the students participate in the *Jelly Roll Squeeze* activity. Have the students stand side by side with their arms around each other's waists. Beginning on one end, tell the students to start to roll toward the other end. The first person should roll toward the second person, the second person should roll toward the third person, the third toward the fourth, on so on. When everyone is curled in, say, "Squeeze" on the count of three.

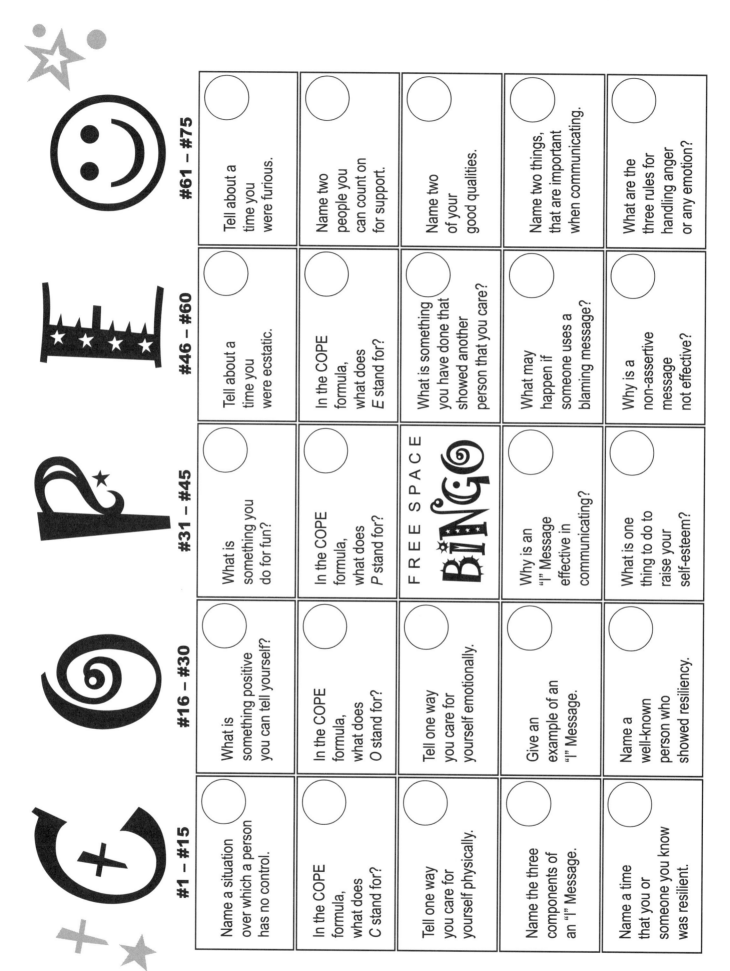

COPE BINGO

C #1–#15	O #16–#30	P #31–#45	E #46–#60	:) #61–#75
Name a situation over which a person has no control.	What is something positive you can tell yourself?	What is something you do for fun?	Tell about a time you were ecstatic.	Tell about a time you were furious.
In the COPE formula, what does C stand for?	In the COPE formula, what does O stand for?	In the COPE formula, what does P stand for?	In the COPE formula, what does E stand for?	Name two people you can count on for support.
Tell one way you care for yourself physically.	Tell one way you care for yourself emotionally.	FREE SPACE BINGO	What is something you have done that showed another person that you care?	Name two of your good qualities.
Name the three components of an "I" Message.	Give an example of an "I" Message.	Why is an "I" Message effective in communicating?	What may happen if someone uses a blaming message?	Name two things, that are important when communicating.
Name a time that you or someone you know was resilient.	Name a well-known person who showed resiliency.	What is one thing to do to raise your self-esteem?	Why is a non-assertive message not effective?	What are the three rules for handling anger or any emotion?

DECISION MAKING

SESSION 1
DECISION-MAKING

Purpose:

To introduce the group members to each other, explain the purpose of the group, and emphasize the importance of good listening skills

Materials Required:

For the leader:
- ☐ *Group Opening* (page 9)
- ☐ *Group Rules* (page 10)
- ☐ Materials for *Energizer 1* (page 13)
- ☐ Materials for *Energizer 2* (page 14)

For each student:
- ☐ 2-pocket manila folder
- ☐ Crayons or markers
- ☐ Pencil

Preparation:

If you have not already done so, reproduce the *Group Rules* and *Group Opening*. Laminate the pages if possible.

Read the instructions for *Energizer 1* and *Energizer 2*. Gather and prepare the necessary materials.

Session Content:

- Introduce the *Group Rules* and the *Group Opening* to the students.

- Explain that the purpose of the group is to learn about different types of decision-making and ways to make better decisions. These skills can make a difference in students' school lives and in their lives as adults.

- Present *Energizer 1*.

- Give each student a folder, crayons or markers, and a pencil. Tell the students the folders will be used to hold their handouts.

- Instruct the students to write their name on the folder, along with the day and class period the group meets. Allow time for the students to use the crayons or markers to decorate their folders.

- Present *Energizer 2* to reinforce the idea that listening to each other while participating in group sessions is very important.

- Collect the folders. (*Note:* The folders will be collected by the leader at the end of each session. At the final session, the students may keep whatever they want from their folders. Shred anything the students do not want to keep.)

SESSION 2
DECISION-MAKING

Purpose:

To identify decisions made in the past week and learn about the three main types of decisions that are made

Materials Required:

For the leader:
- ☐ *Group Opening* (page 9)
- ☐ *Group Rules* (page 10)
- ☐ Materials for *Energizer 4* (page 23)
- ☐ Chalkboard and chalk or dry-erase board and marker

For each student:
- ☐ Student's folder
- ☐ *Five Decisions I Have Made This Week* (page 112)
- ☐ Pencil

Preparation:

Read the instructions for *Energizer 4*. Gather and prepare the necessary materials.

Make a copy of *Five Decisions I Have Made This Week* for each student.

Session Content:

- Give each student his/her folder.

- Select a student to read the *Group Opening*.

- Pass the *Group Rules* around. Have each student read one rule aloud until all of the rules have been read.

- Present *Energizer 4*.

- Give each student a copy of *Five Decisions I Have Made This Week* and a pencil. Have the students complete the activity sheet. Then ask them to share their decisions with the group.

- Explain that there are three main types of decisions:

    Habitual or Automatic
    Example: getting up when the alarm rings, brushing your teeth

    Daily
    Example: deciding what to wear, what to eat

    Major or Life Decision
    Example: deciding where to go to college, where to go to work

- Have the students mark each decision on their activity sheets as:

    A—automatic
    D—daily
    M—major

    Discuss the students' conclusions.

- Write *Emergency Decision* on the board. Ask the students:

    What kind of a decision is this? (An emergency decision must be made quickly and is based on safety.)

    What is an example of an emergency decision? (You see flames coming from the roof of a house and call for help.)

- Have the students put their activity sheets in their folders. Collect the folders.

Directions: After our discussion, go back and mark each decision noting if it was an A—automatic decision, D—daily decision, or M—major decision.

SESSION 3
DECISION-MAKING

Purpose:

To help students learn the five steps of making wise decisions

Materials Required:

For the leader:
- ☐ *Group Opening* (page 9)
- ☐ *Group Rules* (page 10)
- ☐ *Energizer 12* (page 33)

For each student:
- ☐ Student's folder
- ☐ *5 C's In Decision-Making* (page 115)
- ☐ Paper
- ☐ Pencil

Preparation:

Read the instructions for *Energizer 12*.

Make a copy of *5 C's In Decision-Making* for each student.

Session Content:

- Give each student his/her folder.

- Select a student to read the *Group Opening*.

- Pass the *Group Rules* around. Have each student read one rule aloud until all of the rules have been read.

- Present *Energizer 12*.

- Review the concepts of *automatic, daily,* and *major decisions*. Tell the students that *every* decision they make shows who they are and says something about them.

- Give each student a copy of *5 C's In Decision-Making*. Explain the activity sheet in the following way:

    Suppose you had to decide whether to stay up late on a school night and watch your favorite movie or go to bed at your regular time. To do this, you should use the 5 C's In Decision-Making:

    1. Clarify:
    Decide if you want to stay up late to watch your favorite movie.

    2. Consider The Choices:
    Stay up late or go to bed.

    3. Compare And Weigh:
    Pros: will get to see the movie
    Cons: will be tired the next day, may be late to school, may not be able to think clearly

    4. Choose The Best Option:
    Decide to go to bed and rent the movie on the weekend.

    5. Carry Out Your Plan:
    Go to bed.

    After making a decision, it is good to evaluate your choice and the outcome of your decision. Evaluating decisions can help you make wise choices and avoid repeating the same mistakes.

- Ask the students to use the *5 C's In Decision-Making* to determine the best decision for each of the following scenarios:

  1. The class is taking a test. Susie can see Mary's answers. Mary is a good student, and Susie knows that if she copies Mary's answers she will get an A. What is a good decision that Susie can make?

  2. John finds a 20-dollar bill in the hall at school. He decides to keep it because his favorite music group's CD is going on sale today. John heard his friends talking at lunchtime. They say that Joe lost the $20 that his mom gave him to put on his lunch account. What good decision can John make?

  3. The seventh-grade class has been preparing to go on an exciting field trip. The morning of the trip, Jennifer is not feeling well. She really wants to go on the trip. What is a good decision that Jennifer can make?

  4. Maggie is having a birthday party and has invited five of her best friends. Emma promised she would go to the party. Emma's friend Julie just got tickets for a concert the same night as Maggie's party. Julie has asked Emma to go to the concert with her. The concert is being given by Emma's favorite group. What is a good decision Emma can make?

- Give each student paper and a pencil. Have each student write down a situation in which he/she had to make a difficult decision, then present the situation to the group. Tell the students to use the *5 C's In Decision-Making* to come up with the best decision.

- Have the students put their activity sheets in their folders. Collect the folders.

5 C's IN DECISION-MAKING

1

Clarify or define the decision.
Ask yourself: what, where, how, when, why, and whom.

2

Consider the choices.
Look at all the alternatives.

3

Compare and weigh.
Look at all angles, analyze, prioritize.

4

Choose the best option.

5

Carry out your plan.

After making a decision, it is good to evaluate your choice and the outcome of your decision. Evaluating your decisions can help you make wise choices and avoid making the same mistakes over and over again.

SESSION 4
DECISION-MAKING

Purpose:

To explore the differences between simple decisions and complex decisions

Materials Required:

For the leader:
- ☐ *Group Opening* (page 9)
- ☐ *Group Rules* (page 10)
- ☐ Materials for *Energizer 6* (page 25)
- ☐ Chart paper
- ☐ Marker
- ☐ Masking tape

For each student:
- ☐ Student's folder
- ☐ Sticky notes
- ☐ Pencil

For each pair of students:
- ☐ *Simple Decisions/Complex Decisions* (page 118)

Preparation:

Read the instructions for *Energizer 6*. Gather and prepare the necessary materials.

Make a copy of *Simple Decisions/Complex Decisions* for each pair of students.

Title the chart paper *Factors That Can Influence A Decision*. Hang the chart paper on the wall in a location where it can be seen by every student.

Session Content:

- Give each student his/her folder.

- Select a student to read the *Group Opening*.

- Pass the *Group Rules* around. Have each student read one rule aloud until all of the rules have been read.

- Present *Energizer 6*.

- Ask the students:

    What is the difference between a simple decision and a complex decision? (Simple decisions are easy to make. Complex decisions are more difficult to make and may affect others.)

    With complex decisions, you have more alternatives to choose from.

- Have the students form pairs. Give each pair of students a copy of *Simple Decisions/Complex Decisions* and each student a pencil. Tell the students to work together and write down examples of simple decisions they have made and examples of complex decisions they have made. Have each pair of students share its completed activity sheet with the group.

- Review the *5C's In Decision-Making* by saying:

    To make rational and wise decisions, you need to:

- *Understand the problem*
- *Weigh the pros and cons*
- *Avoid "snap" decisions*
- *Consider all possible choices and consequences*
- *Make only "your" decision*
- *Put the "what ifs" aside after the decision is made*
- *Realize that you have choices in your life*

• Point to the chart titled *Factors That Can Influence A Decision*. Give the students sticky notes and ask them to write on the notes factors that can influence a decision.

Some examples are:

values	peers
habits	feelings
family	age
risks	consequences
religion	

Have the students affix their sticky notes to the chart. Discuss the factors the students have written on the sticky notes. Then ask the students to give examples of times when any of these factors affected their decisions.

• Tell the students that they can share at the next session any complex decisions they make between now and then.

• Have the students decide which partner will put the activity sheet in his/her folder. Collect the folders.

SIMPLE DECISIONS/COMPLEX DECISIONS

Directions: Working with a partner, write down some examples of simple decisions and complex decisions.

SIMPLE DECISIONS	COMPLEX DECISIONS

SESSION 5
DECISION-MAKING

Purpose:

To identify the people and things that influence decisions

Materials Required:

For the leader:
- ☐ *Group Opening* (page 9)
- ☐ *Group Rules* (page 10)
- ☐ Materials for *Energizer 3* (page 22)

For each student:
- ☐ Student's folder
- ☐ *Who/What Influences My Decisions* (page 120)
- ☐ Pencil

For each pair of students:
- ☐ *Choosing The Best Decision* (page 121)

Preparation:

Read the instructions for *Energizer 3*. Gather the necessary materials.

Make a copy of *Who/What Influences My Decisions* for each student.

Make a copy of *Choosing The Best Decision* for each pair of students.

Session Content:

- Give each student his/her folder.

- Select a student to read the *Group Opening*.

- Pass the *Group Rules* around. Have each student read one rule aloud until all of the rules have been read.

- Present *Energizer 3*.

- Tell the students that they will be talking about who or what influences their decisions. Give each student a copy of *Who/What Influences My Decisions* and a pencil. Tell the students to complete the activity sheet. Then have the students take turns sharing their thoughts regarding who or what influences the decisions they make.

- Have the students put *Who/What Influences My Decisions* in their folders.

- Have the students form pairs. Give each pair of students a copy of *Choosing The Best Decision*. Review the directions and tell the students to work together and complete the activity sheet. Then have the students share with the group the choices they made.

- Have the students decide which partner will put the *Choosing The Best Decision* activity sheet in his/her folder. Then have the students put their activity sheets in their folders. Collect the folders.

WHO/WHAT INFLUENCES MY DECISIONS

Directions: Fill in the boxes below by writing who or what influences your decisions.

HOME

SCHOOL

FRIENDS

PEER PRESSURE

CHOOSING THE BEST DECISION

Directions: With a partner, complete the activity sheet below using the *5 C's In Decision-Making.* You may refer to the activity sheet in your folder. There are four situations: peer pressure, home, school, and friends. Choose the best decision for each situation.

Peer Pressure
Your friends want you to snub a new student at lunchtime. You told your school counselor that you would eat lunch with the new student. Using the *5C's In Decision-Making*, what will you decide to do?

_____
_____
_____

Home
Your mother told you to be sure to get home right after school and do your homework because you have basketball practice after supper. When you get home, you feel tired and want to have fun playing your new videogame. Using the *5C's In Decision-Making*, what will you decide to do?

_____
_____
_____

School
You are doing poorly in math and need to raise your grade. Your math teacher has offered to stay after school on Wednesday for a help session. You have a Chess Club meeting at the same time. Using the *5C's In Decision-Making*, what will you decide to do?

_____
_____
_____

Friends
One of your friends always talks badly about your other friend in front of you. This not only upsets you, but puts you in the middle. Using the *5C's In Decision-Making*, what will you decide to do?

_____
_____
_____

SESSION 6
DECISION-MAKING

Purpose:

To give students experience in making a group decision

Materials Required:

For the leader:
- ☐ *Group Opening* (page 9)
- ☐ *Group Rules* (page 10)
- ☐ Materials for *Energizer 5* (page 24)
- ☐ Chart paper
- ☐ Marker
- ☐ Masking tape

For each student:
- ☐ Student's folder
- ☐ Sticky notes
- ☐ Pencil

For the student group's leader:
- ☐ *Camping Trip* (page 124)

Preparation:

Read the instructions for *Energizer 5*. Gather and prepare the necessary materials.

Title the chart paper *Group Decisions*. Display the chart on a wall in the room.

Make one copy of *Camping Trip*.

Session Content:

- Give each student his/her folder.

- Select a student to read the *Group Opening*.

- Pass the *Group Rules* around. Have each student read one rule aloud until all of the rules have been read.

- Present *Energizer 5*.

- Tell the students that today's lesson is about group decisions. Explain that a group decision could be when the class votes to take the test on Wednesday instead of Friday or a majority of friends decides to see a certain movie.

- Point to the chart titled *Group Decisions*. Give each student sticky notes and a pencil. Tell the students to write about one or more times that they have participated in a group decision. Have the students post their notes on the chart. Discuss what is written on the notes by asking:

    Was this the best decision?

    Did it work?

- Tell the students:

    In most cases, you have no choice once a group decision has been made. For example, the class who voted to take the test on Wednesday. As long as the decision is safe and healthy, you go along with the group. Of course, if the group decision is unsafe or unhealthy, it is best not to give in to peer pressure and to not go along with the group decision.

- Involve the students in making a group decision. Say:

I am going to ask you to work together and make group decisions. First, you must pick a leader. The leader will make sure that everyone has a fair chance to speak and that everyone will be listened to. Once you have chosen a leader, you will work as a group to reach an agreement on how to respond to the questions on the activity sheet. When you have completed the activity sheet, I will listen to your results and ask you questions about how you reached your decisions.

- Have the students select a group leader.

- Give a copy of *Camping Trip* to the group's leader. Tell the students how much time they have to complete the activity sheet. When the allotted time has elapsed, ask the following questions:

    Did each of you give input?

    Did you feel you were listened to?

    Did you make the decisions as a group or did certain people make them?

    What obstacles did you run into?

    Did anyone disagree with one of the decisions? If so, how was that handled?

    What did you enjoy about making a group decision?

    Was it difficult to make a group decision?

    Is there anything else anyone would like to add?

- Have the students talk about the advantages and disadvantages of group decisions.

- Conclude the session by asking each group member whether he/she prefers group decisions or individual decisions.

- Have the group leader put the *Camping Trip* activity sheet in his/her folder. Collect the folders.

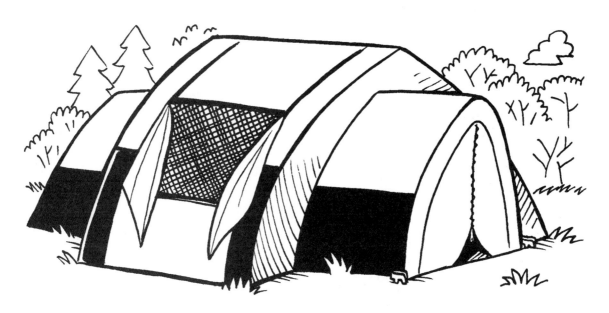

CAMPING TRIP

Directions: Your group has been given an all-expense-paid trip to a camp in the mountains! There is one catch: There is no electricity at the camp. Decide the following:

When will you go? _____

How will you get there? _____

What will you bring? _____
_____
_____
_____
_____

What will you do? _____
_____
_____
_____
_____

How long will you stay? _____

You may bring two adults with you. Who will they be? _____
_____

Describe your trip using one word. What is the word? _____

SESSION 7
DECISION-MAKING

Purpose:

To help students evaluate decisions that have already been made

Materials Required:

For the leader:
- ☐ *Group Opening* (page 9)
- ☐ *Group Rules* (page 10)
- ☐ Materials for *Energizer 7* (page 30)

For each student:
- ☐ Student's folder
- ☐ *Decisions I Have Made* (page 126)
- ☐ Pencil

Preparation:

Read the instructions for *Energizer 7*. Gather and prepare the necessary materials.

Make a copy of *Decisions I Have Made* for each student.

Session Content:

- Give each student his/her folder.

- Select a student to read the *Group Opening*.

- Pass the *Group Rules* around. Have each student read one rule aloud until all of the rules have been read.

- Present *Energizer 7*.

- Give each student a copy of *Decisions I Have Made* and a pencil. Tell the students to complete the activity sheet. Then have the students share their answers with the group, explaining why they made the decision and what went right or wrong.

- Have the students put their activity sheets in their folders. Collect the folders.

GRAB BAG GUIDANCE © 2005 MAR*CO PRODUCTS, INC. 1-800-448-2197

Decisions I Have Made??

A good decision I made was _____
_____.

Another good decision I made was _____
_____.

The best decision I ever made was _____
_____.

A poor decision I made was_____
_____.

Another poor decision I made was _____
_____.

The worst decision I ever made was _____
_____.

The hardest decision I ever made was _____
_____.

The easiest decision I ever made was _____
_____.

A decision I wish I could change is _____
_____.

A major decision that I will have to make in the near future is _____
_____.

SESSION 8
DECISION-MAKING

Purpose:

To have students use the *5 C's In Decision-Making Chart* to make a decision

Materials Required:

For the leader:
- ☐ *Group Opening* (page 9)
- ☐ *Group Rules* (page 10)
- ☐ *Energizer 9* (page 31)
- ☐ Chalkboard and chalk or dry-erase board and marker

Preparation:

Read the instructions for *Energizer 9*.

Session Content:

- Give each student his/her folder.

- Select a student to read the *Group Opening*.

- Pass the *Group Rules* around. Have each student read one rule aloud until all of the rules have been read.

- Present *Energizer 9*.

- Tell the students:

    Decision-making often involves choosing how to spend money. Using the 5 C's In Decision-Making chart in your folder, describe how you would decide to spend $50.00.

- Guide the students through the process as follows:

    1. **Clarify**: You have $50.00 to spend

    2. **Consider The Choices**: Video game, shoes, radio, movie and out to eat

    3. **Compare And Weigh**: Do my parents agree? Is it long-lasting? Can I use it with other things? Can I use it year-round?

    4. **Choose The Best Option**

    5. **Carry Out Your Plan**

- Tell the students that sometimes they can *compare and weigh* by using a chart. Draw the chart (below) on the board, using a plus (+) if the students' answer is *yes*, and a minus (−) if the students' answer is *no*.

CHOICES	PARENTS APPROVAL	LONG LASTING	USE WITH OTHER THINGS	USE YEAR ROUND
Videogame	+	−	−	+
Shoes	+	+	+	+
Radio	+	+	+	+
Movie and Dinner	+	−	−	−

- Tell the students:

    Looking at the pluses and minuses, you can decide which is the best way to spend your money. You can do this by looking for the most positives.

- Conclude the session by having the students give other examples of how the money can be spent. Chart their responses.

- Collect the folders.

SESSION 9
DECISION-MAKING

Purpose:

To review what has been presented in previous lessons

Materials Required:

For the leader:
- ☐ *Group Opening* (page 9)
- ☐ *Group Rules* (page 10)
- ☐ Materials for *Energizer 10* (page 32)
- ☐ *Bingo Numbers* (pages 42-43)
- ☐ Container

For each student:
- ☐ Student's folder
- ☐ *Decision-Making Bingo* (page 130)
- ☐ Markers or pens of two different-color inks

Preparation:

Read the instructions for *Energizer 10*. Gather the necessary materials.

Make a copy of *Decision-Making Bingo* for each student.

Make a copy of the *Bingo Numbers*. Cut the numbers apart and place them in the container.

Session Content:

- Give each student his/her folder.

- Select a student to read the *Group Opening*.

- Pass the *Group Rules* around. Have each student read one rule aloud until all of the rules have been read.

- Present *Energizer 10*.

- Tell the students:

    This is our last session. Before we end this session, we are going to play Decision-Making Bingo. *As we play this game, we will review things we have learned in the past few weeks.*

- Give each student a copy of *Decision-Making Bingo* and markers or pens of two different-color inks. Explain how the students should fill in their bingo cards by saying:

    The letters DE C I D E *are printed at the top of the columns. Below each letter is a number range. Using one color of ink/marker, fill in each circle in each column with one of the numbers within the indicated range. For example, you may choose 3, 5, 8, 12, and 15 to fill in the circles in the column under the letters* DE.

- Explain how the game is played by saying:

    I will draw one number at a time from this container. As I draw each number, look at your Decision-Making Bingo *card to see if you have written that number on your card. If you have that number on your card, raise your hand. I will call on you to complete the sentence written in that space. You may then place an X in the box using the other color of ink/marker. The first person to get five X's in a row should call out* Decision-Making Bingo! *He or she will win the game.*

- Play the game.

- Discuss the statements on the *Decision-Making Bingo* cards. Ask the students which were easy to complete and which were difficult.

- Have the students go through their folders and give you any papers they want shredded. They may keep their folders and any papers they want.

- To conclude the group, have the students participate in the *Jelly Roll Squeeze* activity. Have the students stand side by side with their arms around each other's waists. Beginning on one end, tell the students to start to roll toward the other end. The first person should roll toward the second person, the second person should roll toward the third person, the third toward the fourth, on so on. When everyone is curled in, say, "Squeeze" on the count of three.

- Thank the students for participating in the group and for sharing with others.

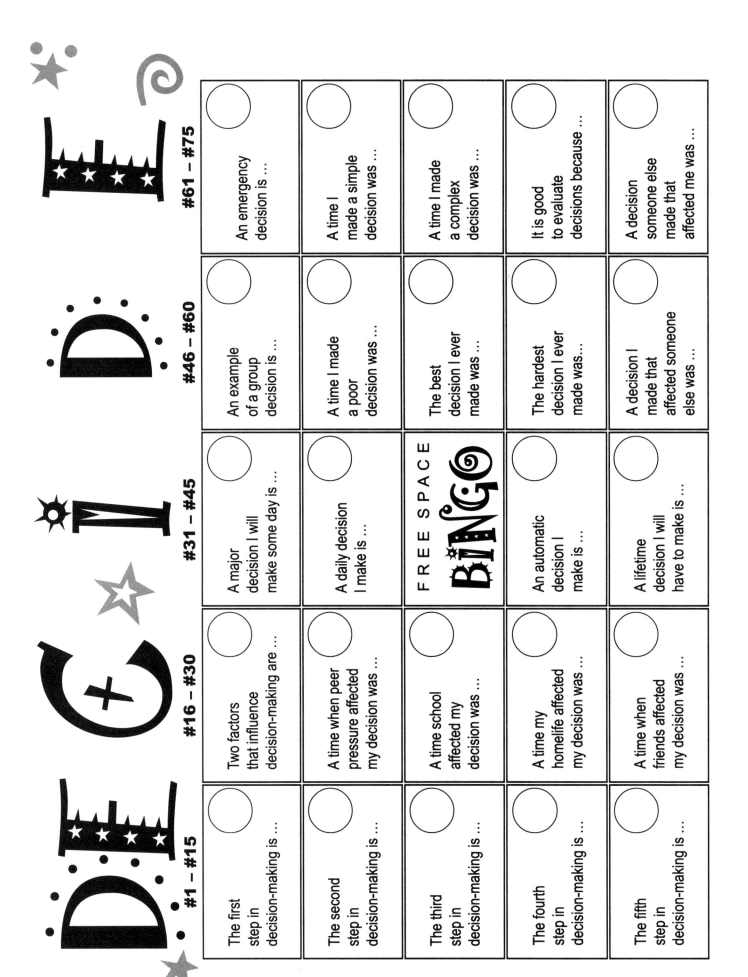

DIVORCE

SESSION 1
DIVORCE

Purpose:

To introduce the group members to each other, explain the purpose of the group, and emphasize the importance of good listening skills

Materials Required:

For the leader:
- ☐ *Group Opening* (page 9)
- ☐ *Group Rules* (page 10)
- ☐ Materials for *Energizer 1* (page 13)
- ☐ Materials for *Energizer 2* (page 14)

For each student:
- ☐ 2-pocket manila folder
- ☐ Crayons or markers
- ☐ Pencil

Preparation:

If you have not already done so, reproduce the *Group Rules* and *Group Opening*. Laminate the pages if possible.

Read the instructions for *Energizer 1* and *Energizer 2*. Gather and prepare the necessary materials.

Session Content:

- Introduce the *Group Rules* and the *Group Opening* to the students.

- Explain that the purpose of the group is to discuss divorce and how it relates to the group members' personal situations.

- Present *Energizer 1*.

- Give each student a folder, crayons or markers, and a pencil. Tell the students the folders will be used to hold their handouts.

- Instruct the students to write their name on the folder, along with the day and class period the group meets. Allow time for the students to use the crayons or markers to decorate their folders.

- Present *Energizer 2* to reinforce the idea that listening to each other while participating in the sessions is very important.

- Collect the folders. (*Note:* The folders will be collected by the leader at the end of each session. At the final session, the students may keep whatever they want from their folders. Shred anything the students do not want to keep.)

SESSION 2
DIVORCE

Purpose:

To help the students become better acquainted with each other and provide insight into their personal thoughts about their families

Materials Required:

For the leader:
- ☐ *Group Opening* (page 9)
- ☐ *Group Rules* (page 10)
- ☐ Materials for *Energizer 3* (page 22)
- ☐ Piece of art paper
- ☐ Pencil

For each student:
- ☐ Student's folder
- ☐ Piece of art paper
- ☐ Pencil

Preparation:

Read the instructions for *Energizer 3*. Gather the necessary materials.

Following the directions for the session, draw a picture of your family to show the students.

Session Content:

- Give each student his/her folder.

- Select a student to read the *Group Opening*.

- Pass the *Group Rules* around. Have each student read one rule aloud until all of the rules have been read.

- Present *Energizer 3*.

- Show the students the picture of your family. Give each student a piece of art paper and a pencil. Then say:

  Using circles, draw a picture of your family. Draw a circle to represent each family member. In each circle, write the initials of the person that circle represents. If you believe family members have a close relationship, draw their circles close to each other. If you believe family members do not have a close relationship, draw their circles farther apart. At the bottom of the paper, write three words that describe your mother, your father, and yourself.

- Have each student talk about his/her picture.

- Have the students put their pictures in their folders. Collect the folders.

SESSION 3
DIVORCE

Purpose:

To have the students evaluate their feelings about their parents' divorce/separation

Materials Required:

For the leader:
- ☐ *Group Opening* (page 9)
- ☐ *Group Rules* (page 10)
- ☐ *Energizer 9* (page 31)

For each student:
- ☐ Student's folder
- ☐ *Incomplete Sentences* (page 135)
- ☐ Pencil

Preparation:

Read the instructions for *Energizer 9*.

Make a copy of *Incomplete Sentences* for each student.

Session Content:

- Give each student his/her folder.

- Select a student to read the *Group Opening*.

- Pass the *Group Rules* around. Have each student read one rule aloud until all of the rules have been read.

- Present *Energizer 9*.

- Give each student a copy of *Incomplete Sentences* and a pencil. Tell the students to complete the activity sheet by relating their answers to their parents' divorce/separation. Discuss each sentence and the students' answers.

- Have the students put their activity sheets in their folders. Collect the folders.

INCOMPLETE SENTENCES

1. My parents have been divorced/separated (how long) _____.
2. I live with _____.
3. I am not okay with _____ _____.
4. The holidays are _____ _____.
5. My friends think _____ _____.
6. Something that I would like to change is _____ _____.
7. Something that I like about the divorce/separation is _____ _____.
8. Something that I dislike about the divorce/separation is _____ _____.
9. My mom _____ _____.
10. My dad _____ _____.
11. I am sorry _____ _____.
12. Sometimes I am afraid that _____ _____.
13. I often worry _____ _____.
14. I think _____ _____.
15. My dream is _____ _____.

SESSION 4
DIVORCE

Purpose:

To determine the level of difficulty facing the students in various divorce situations

Materials Required:

For the leader:
- ☐ *Group Opening* (page 9)
- ☐ *Group Rules* (page 10)
- ☐ Materials for *Energizer 5* (page 24)
- ☐ Yellow and blue paper or cardstock
- ☐ *Difficult Divorce Cards* (page 137)
- ☐ *Not Difficult Divorce Cards* (page 138)
- ☐ *Difficult/Not Difficult Sentences* (page 139)

Preparation:

Read the instructions for *Energizer 5*. Gather and prepare the necessary materials.

Make a copy of the *Difficult Divorce Cards* on yellow paper/cardstock. Make a copy of the *Not Difficult Divorce Cards* on blue paper/cardstock. Cut the cards apart.

Make a copy of the *Difficult/Not Difficult Sentences.*

Session Content:

- Select a student to read the *Group Opening.*

- Pass the *Group Rules* around. Have each student read one rule aloud until all of the rules have been read.

- Present *Energizer 5.*

- Give each student a *Difficult Divorce Card* and a *Not Difficult Divorce Card.*

- Read aloud each *Difficult/Not Difficult Sentence.* After you have read each sentence, the students will hold up either a yellow or blue card, depending on whether the situation described in the sentence is difficult or not difficult for them. Discuss each statement before reading the next one.

- Conclude the session by asking the students to raise their hands if they felt there were more difficult situations or more not difficult situations.

DIFFICULT	DIFFICULT
GRAB BAG GUIDANCE: DIFFICULT DIVORCE CARDS © 2005 MAR*CO PRODUCTS, INC. 1-800-448-2197	GRAB BAG GUIDANCE: DIFFICULT DIVORCE CARDS © 2005 MAR*CO PRODUCTS, INC. 1-800-448-2197
DIFFICULT	DIFFICULT
GRAB BAG GUIDANCE: DIFFICULT DIVORCE CARDS © 2005 MAR*CO PRODUCTS, INC. 1-800-448-2197	GRAB BAG GUIDANCE: DIFFICULT DIVORCE CARDS © 2005 MAR*CO PRODUCTS, INC. 1-800-448-2197
DIFFICULT	DIFFICULT
GRAB BAG GUIDANCE: DIFFICULT DIVORCE CARDS © 2005 MAR*CO PRODUCTS, INC. 1-800-448-2197	GRAB BAG GUIDANCE: DIFFICULT DIVORCE CARDS © 2005 MAR*CO PRODUCTS, INC. 1-800-448-2197
DIFFICULT	DIFFICULT
GRAB BAG GUIDANCE: DIFFICULT DIVORCE CARDS © 2005 MAR*CO PRODUCTS, INC. 1-800-448-2197	GRAB BAG GUIDANCE: DIFFICULT DIVORCE CARDS © 2005 MAR*CO PRODUCTS, INC. 1-800-448-2197
DIFFICULT	DIFFICULT
GRAB BAG GUIDANCE: DIFFICULT DIVORCE CARDS © 2005 MAR*CO PRODUCTS, INC. 1-800-448-2197	GRAB BAG GUIDANCE: DIFFICULT DIVORCE CARDS © 2005 MAR*CO PRODUCTS, INC. 1-800-448-2197

NOT DIFFICULT	**NOT DIFFICULT**
GRAB BAG GUIDANCE: NOT DIFFICULT DIVORCE CARDS © 2005 MAR✶CO PRODUCTS, INC. 1-800-448-2197	GRAB BAG GUIDANCE: NOT DIFFICULT DIVORCE CARDS © 2005 MAR✶CO PRODUCTS, INC. 1-800-448-2197
NOT DIFFICULT	**NOT DIFFICULT**
GRAB BAG GUIDANCE: NOT DIFFICULT DIVORCE CARDS © 2005 MAR✶CO PRODUCTS, INC. 1-800-448-2197	GRAB BAG GUIDANCE: NOT DIFFICULT DIVORCE CARDS © 2005 MAR✶CO PRODUCTS, INC. 1-800-448-2197
NOT DIFFICULT	**NOT DIFFICULT**
GRAB BAG GUIDANCE: NOT DIFFICULT DIVORCE CARDS © 2005 MAR✶CO PRODUCTS, INC. 1-800-448-2197	GRAB BAG GUIDANCE: NOT DIFFICULT DIVORCE CARDS © 2005 MAR✶CO PRODUCTS, INC. 1-800-448-2197
NOT DIFFICULT	**NOT DIFFICULT**
GRAB BAG GUIDANCE: NOT DIFFICULT DIVORCE CARDS © 2005 MAR✶CO PRODUCTS, INC. 1-800-448-2197	GRAB BAG GUIDANCE: NOT DIFFICULT DIVORCE CARDS © 2005 MAR✶CO PRODUCTS, INC. 1-800-448-2197
NOT DIFFICULT	**NOT DIFFICULT**
GRAB BAG GUIDANCE: NOT DIFFICULT DIVORCE CARDS © 2005 MAR✶CO PRODUCTS, INC. 1-800-448-2197	GRAB BAG GUIDANCE: NOT DIFFICULT DIVORCE CARDS © 2005 MAR✶CO PRODUCTS, INC. 1-800-448-2197

DIFFICULT/NOT DIFFICULT SENTENCES

My parents are divorced.

I live with my mom.

I live with my dad.

I live with my siblings.

I have had to move.

I spend time with the parent I don't live with.

There have been changes since my parents' divorce.

My parents fight a lot.

Sometimes, I blame myself for my parents' fighting.

My mom/dad uses me to carry messages back and forth.

I got to choose the parent I live with.

I miss the parent that I don't live with.

My parents tell me unkind things about each other.

My mother/father has remarried (state which one).

I have stepsiblings.

My friends are supportive of me.

We have had money problems since my parents divorced.

I spend the holidays with both parents.

Sometimes I worry about hurting the feelings of the parent I don't live with.

Sometimes I am afraid to tell my mom or dad how I feel.

I worry about what my friends think about my parents being divorced.

I feel better since my parents divorced.

I worry about "court battles" over visitation.

My grades/schoolwork have been affected by my parents' divorce.

I miss relatives, such as grandparents, of the parent I don't live with.

SESSION 5
DIVORCE

Purpose:

To identify the divorce-related situations that worry the students and make note of those situations they can control and those over which they have no control

Materials Required:

For the leader:
- ☐ *Group Opening* (page 9)
- ☐ *Group Rules* (page 10)
- ☐ Materials for *Energizer 6* (page 25)

For each student:
- ☐ Student's folder
- ☐ *Things I Worry About* (page 141)
- ☐ Pencil

Preparation:

Read the instructions for *Energizer 6*. Gather and prepare the necessary materials.

Make a copy of *Things I Worry About* for each student.

Session Content:

- Give each student his/her folder.

- Select a student to read the *Group Opening*.

- Pass the *Group Rules* around. Have each student read one rule aloud until all of the rules have been read.

- Present *Energizer 6*.

- Give each student a copy of *Things I Worry About* and a pencil. Have the students complete the activity sheet. Discuss their conclusions.

- Ask the students:

    If you have no control over a situation, why do you suppose it worries you? (Accept all answers.)

    Do you believe it helps to worry about something you cannot control? (No.)

    Do you believe you can stop worrying about something you cannot control? (Probably not.) *Why do you think this is so?* (Because you care about the situation and wish you could do something about it.)

    If you can't stop worrying about something you cannot control, what is the best thing you can do? (Be concerned about the situation, but realize that whatever happens is out of your control.)

- Tell the students that when they start to worry they should think about whether they have any control over the situation that is worrying them. If they have control over the situation, tell them to take appropriate action. If they do not have control over the situation, tell them to realize that even though they may worry, the end result is out of their hands.

- Have the students put their activity sheets in their folders. Collect the folders.

THINGS I WORRY ABOUT

THINGS I HAVE WORRIED ABOUT SINCE MY PARENTS' DIVORCE/SEPARATION:

☐ _____

☐ _____

☐ _____

☐ _____

☐ _____

☐ _____

☐ _____

☐ _____

☐ _____

☐ _____

☐ _____

Put a checkmark (✔) beside those things over which you have control.

SESSION 6
DIVORCE

Purpose

To help students verbalize the best and worst things about their parents' divorce and analyze the changes seen in family and friends

Materials Required:

For the leader:
- ☐ *Group Opening* (page 9)
- ☐ *Group Rules* (page 10)
- ☐ Materials for *Energizer 7* (page 30)

For each student:
- ☐ Student's folder
- ☐ Piece of white unlined paper
- ☐ Pencil
- ☐ Scissors
- ☐ *Family Changes* (page 143)

Preparation:

Read the instructions for *Energizer 7*. Gather and prepare the necessary materials.

Make a copy of *Family Changes* for each student.

Session Content:

- Give each student his/her folder.

- Select a student to read the *Group Opening*.

- Pass the *Group Rules* around. Have each student read one rule aloud until all of the rules have been read.

- Present *Energizer 7*.

- Give each student a piece of white unlined paper, pencil, and a pair of scissors. Then say:

    Draw a large heart on the paper, then cut it out. Divide the heart in half. On one half of the heart, write "Best." On the other half, write "Worst." Then write about the best and worst things that have happened since your parents' divorce/separation.

    Have the students share their written comments with the group.

- Give each student a copy of *Family Changes*. Tell the students to complete the activity sheet. Discuss what the students have written.

- Have the students put their activity sheets in their folders. Collect the folders.

FAMILY CHANGES

Directions: List the way each person(s) has changed since your parents' divorce/separation.

MY MOM
_____
_____
_____
_____
_____
_____

MY DAD
_____
_____
_____
_____
_____
_____

MY SIBLINGS
_____
_____
_____
_____
_____
_____

MYSELF
_____
_____
_____
_____
_____
_____

MY GRANDPARENTS
_____
_____
_____
_____
_____
_____

MY FRIENDS
_____
_____
_____
_____
_____
_____

SESSION 7
DIVORCE

Purpose:

To encourage the students to express their feelings about the divorce/separation and related situations

Materials Required:

For the leader:
- ☐ *Group Opening* (page 9)
- ☐ *Group Rules* (page 10)
- ☐ *Energizer 13* (page 33)
- ☐ Chalkboard and chalk or dry-erase board and marker

For each student:
- ☐ Student's folder
- ☐ *Secret Thoughts* (page 145)
- ☐ Pencil
- ☐ Piece of paper

Preparation:

Read the instructions for *Energizer 13*.

Make a copy of the *Secret Thoughts* for each student.

Session Content:

- Give each student his/her folder.

- Select a student to read the *Group Opening*.

- Pass the *Group Rules* around. Have each student read one rule aloud until all of the rules have been read.

- Present *Energizer 13*.

- Give each student a copy of *Secret Thoughts* and a pencil. Tell the students to complete the activity sheet. Have the students share their answers with the group.

- Go to the board and write the following:

    D
    I
    V
    O
    R
    C
    E

    Working together, have the group members think of words that describe feelings associated with divorce that begin with each letter in the word *DIVORCE*.

    For example:

    D   disappointed, discouraged
    I   innocent
    V   vicious, vulnerable
    O   overworked
    R   regret, relief
    C   confused, curious
    E   embarrassed, exhausted

- Give each student a piece of paper. Have each student select one word listed on the board that best describes his/her feelings about divorce. If the word the student wishes to use is not listed, he/she may choose another word. On the piece of paper, have the students complete the following sentence:

    The word that best describes my feeling about divorce is _____ , because _____ .

- Have the students put their activity sheets in their folders. Collect the folders.

SECRET THOUGHTS

If I could change one thing about my parent's divorce, it would be …	I wish I could tell my dad …
What bothers me most is …	I wish I could tell my mom …
Something I am afraid of is …	Something I am content with is …
A good memory I have of my family is …	A bad memory I have of my family is …

SESSION 8
DIVORCE

Purpose:

To help students examine their feelings about their parents' divorce/separation

Materials Required:

For the leader:
- ☐ *Group Opening* (page 9)
- ☐ *Group Rules* (page 10)
- ☐ Materials for *Energizer 4* (page 23)
- ☐ *Divorce Situations* (page 148)
- ☐ Scissors
- ☐ Container

For each student:
- ☐ Student's folder
- ☐ *Feelings Thermometer* (page 147)
- ☐ 5 crayons or markers of different colors

Preparation:

Read the instructions for *Energizer 4*. Gather and prepare the necessary materials.

Make a copy of *Feelings Thermometer* for each student.

Make a copy of *Divorce Situations*. Cut the strips apart and place them in the container.

Session Content:

- Give each student his/her folder.

- Select a student to read the *Group Opening*.

- Pass the *Group Rules* around. Have each student read one rule aloud until all of the rules have been read.

- Present *Energizer 4*.

- Give each student a copy of *Feelings Thermometer* and 5 different-color crayons or markers. Tell the students to complete the activity sheet. Have the students share the completed activity sheets with the group.

- Have the students draw the *Divorce Situations* strips from the container. Have each student talk about how he/she would handle the situation described on the strip.

- Have the students put their activity sheets in their folders. Collect the folders.

FEELINGS THERMOMETER

Directions: Select five colors to represent five feelings you have about your parents' divorce/separation. Starting at the bottom of the thermometer, fill in the first section with the color representing your least-intense feeling. Continue up the thermometer, filling in the sections. The color at the top of the thermometer should represent your most-intense feeling.

FEELING **COLOR REPRESENTING THE FEELING**

1. _____   _____
2. _____   _____
3. _____   _____
4. _____   _____
5. _____   _____

Divorce Situations

Directions: Cut apart the strips and place them in a container.

What would you do if your friend told you that his/her parents were getting a divorce?

What would you do if you wanted to live with your other parent?

What would you do if one of your parents put the other parent down?

What would you do if you didn't like the person your parent was dating?

What would you do if one of your parents always wanted you to give messages to the other parent?

What would you do if your sibling wanted to live with your non-custodial parent?

What would you do if your custodial parent wouldn't let you see your non-custodial parent's relatives?

What would you like to tell the judge?

What would you do if you did not have any input about where you spend the holidays?

SESSION 9
DIVORCE

Purpose:

To review what has been presented in previous lessons

Materials Required:

For the leader:
- ☐ *Group Opening* (page 9)
- ☐ *Group Rules* (page 10)
- ☐ *Energizer 15* (page 34)
- ☐ *Bingo Numbers* (pages 42-43)
- ☐ Container

For each student:
- ☐ Student's folder
- ☐ *Divorce Bingo* (page 151)
- ☐ Markers or pens of two different-color inks

Preparation:

Read the instructions for *Energizer 15*.

Make a copy of *Divorce Bingo* for each student.

Make a copy of the *Bingo Numbers*. Cut the numbers apart and place them in the container.

Session Content:

- Give each student his/her folder.

- Select a student to read the *Group Opening*.

- Pass the *Group Rules* around. Have each student read one rule aloud until all of the rules have been read.

- Present *Energizer 15*.

- Tell the students:

    We are going to play Divorce Bingo. *As we play this game, we will review things we have learned in the past few weeks.*

- Give each student a copy of *Divorce Bingo* and markers or pens of two different-color inks. Explain how the students should fill in their bingo cards by saying:

    The letters DI V O R CE *are printed at the top of the columns. Below each letter is a number range. Using one color of ink/marker, fill in each circle in each column with one of the numbers within the indicated range. For example, you may choose 3, 5, 8, 12, and 15 to fill in the circles in the column under the letters* DI.

- Explain how the game is played by saying:

    I will draw one number at a time from this container. As I draw each number, look at your Divorce Bingo *card to see if you have written that number on your card. If you have that number on your card, raise your hand. I will call on you to complete the sentence* written in that space. You may then place an X in the box using the other color of ink/marker. The first person to get five X's in a row should call out *Divorce Bingo!* He or she will win the game.

- Play the game.

- Discuss the statements on the *Divorce Bingo* cards. Ask the students which were easy to complete and which were difficult.

- Have the students put their bingo cards in their folders. Collect the folders.

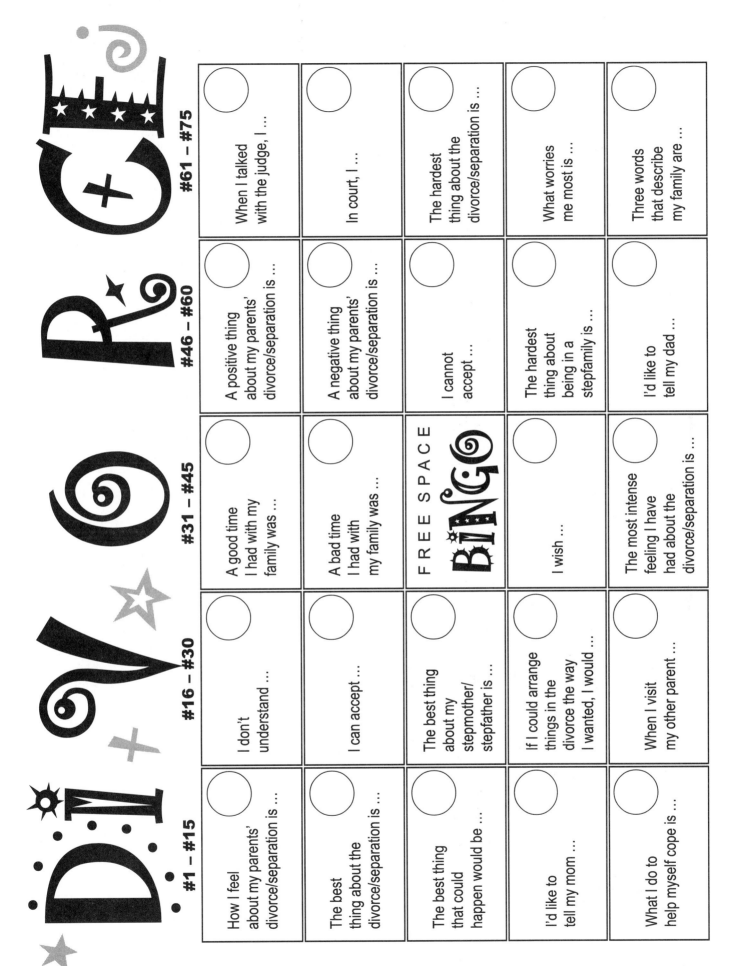

SESSION 10
DIVORCE

Purpose:

To bring closure to the group

Materials Required:

For the leader:
- ☐ *Group Opening* (page 9)
- ☐ *Group Rules* (page 10)
- ☐ Materials for *Energizer 10* (page 32)

For each student:
- ☐ Student's folder
- ☐ Index card
- ☐ Pencil

Preparation:

Read the instructions for *Energizer 10*. Gather the necessary materials.

Session Content:

- Give each student his/her folder.

- Select a student to read the *Group Opening*.

- Pass the *Group Rules* around. Have each student read one rule aloud until all of the rules have been read.

- Present *Energizer 10*.

- Give each student an index card and a pencil. Have each student list his/her hopes for the future and state how those hopes will be achieved. Then have the students share their hopes with the group.

- Remind them they did not cause their parents' divorce/separation. Tell the students that, hopefully, the activities they experienced in group will help them cope more effectively with the situation.

- Have the students go through their folders and give you any papers they want shredded. They may keep their folders and any papers they want.

- To conclude the group, have the students participate in the *Jelly Roll Squeeze* activity. Have the students stand side by side with their arms around each other's waists. Beginning on one end, tell the students to start to roll toward the other end. The first person should roll toward the second person, the second person should roll toward the third person, the third toward the fourth, on so on. When everyone is curled in, say, "Squeeze" on the count of three.

- Thank the students for participating in the group and for sharing with others.

Grief & Loss

SESSION 1
GRIEF AND LOSS

Purpose:

To introduce the group members to each other, explain the purpose of the group, and emphasize the importance of good listening skills

Materials Required:

For the leader:
- ☐ *Group Opening* (page 9)
- ☐ *Group Rules* (page 10)
- ☐ Materials for *Energizer 1* (page 13)
- ☐ Materials for *Energizer 2* (page 14)

For each student:
- ☐ 2-pocket manila folder
- ☐ Crayons or markers
- ☐ Pencil

Preparation:

If you have not already done so, reproduce the *Group Rules* and *Group Opening*. Laminate the pages if possible.

Read the instructions for *Energizer 1* and *Energizer 2*. Gather and prepare the necessary materials.

Session Content:

- Introduce the *Group Rules* and the *Group Opening* to the students.

- Explain that the purpose of the group is to discuss *loss* and how that subject relates to their personal situations.

- Present *Energizer 1*.

- Give each student a folder, crayons or markers, and a pencil. Tell the students the folders will be used to hold their handouts.

- Instruct the students to write their name on the folder, along with the day and class period the group meets. Allow time for the students to use the crayons or markers to decorate their folders.

- Present *Energizer 2* to reinforce the concept that listening to each other while participating in group sessions is very important.

- Collect the folders. (*Note:* The folders will be collected by the leader at the end of each session. At the final session, the students may keep whatever they want from their folders. Shred anything the students do not want to keep.)

SESSION 2
GRIEF AND LOSS

Purpose:

To enable students to become more familiar with each other and provide insight into their personal thoughts about their families

Materials Required:

For the leader:
- ☐ *Group Opening* (page 9)
- ☐ *Group Rules* (page 10)
- ☐ Materials for *Energizer 4* (page 23)
- ☐ Chalkboard and chalk or dry-erase board and marker

For each student:
- ☐ Student's folder
- ☐ Paper
- ☐ Pencil

Preparation:

Read the instructions for *Energizer 4*. Gather and prepare the necessary materials.

Session Content:

- Give each student his/her folder.

- Select a student to read the *Group Opening*.

- Pass the *Group Rules* around. Have each student read one rule aloud until all of the rules have been read.

- Present *Energizer 4*.

- Explain the following to the students:

Whenever you feel like someone or something is missing from your life, you experience loss. This occurs not only when someone dies, but also when a friend moves away or you move away from friends. You can feel loss when a pet dies or parents divorce.

- Give each student paper and a pencil. Tell the students to make a list of people or pets they had in their life and have lost. Have the students share their lists with the group.

- Have the students brainstorm about feeling words associated with grief. Write the students' suggestions on the board as they are mentioned. Discuss each word, reminding the students that there are no good or bad feelings. Everyone may not feel the same way, and that is okay. The important thing is for the students to experience their feelings.

Examples of feeling words associated with grief:

confused	hurt	sad
nervous	angry	alone
different	frustrated	lonely
depressed	scared	annoyed
emotional	withdrawn	worried
anxious	miserable	betrayed

- Quickly review the words on the board by asking the students to raise their hands if they have ever had any of these feelings when experiencing loss.

- Have the students put their papers in their folders. Collect the folders.

SESSION 3
GRIEF AND LOSS

Purpose:

To visually represent the differences in each student's family as a result of loss

Materials Required:

For the leader:
- ☐ *Group Opening* (page 9)
- ☐ *Group Rules* (page 10)
- ☐ Materials for *Energizer 5* (page 24)
- ☐ Piece of white art paper
- ☐ Pencil

For each student:
- ☐ Student's folder
- ☐ Piece of white art paper
- ☐ Pencil

Preparation:

Read the instructions for *Energizer 5*. Gather and prepare the necessary materials.

Following the directions in the session, draw a "now" and "then" picture of your family to show the students.

Session Content:

- Give each student his/her folder.

- Select a student to read the *Group Opening*.

- Pass the *Group Rules* around. Have each student read one rule aloud until all of the rules have been read.

- Present *Energizer 5*.

- Give each student a piece of art paper and a pencil. Tell the students to divide their paper in half by drawing a vertical line down the middle. Then say:

    On each half of your paper, I want you to draw a picture of your family. On the left side, draw a picture of your family when your loved one was with you. On the right side, draw a picture of your family now. Draw a circle to represent each family member. In each circle, write the initials of the person that circle represents. If you believe family members have or have had a close relationship, draw their circles close to each other. If you believe family members do not or did not have a close relationship, draw their circles farther apart.

    When you have completed your drawing, write three feeling words in your "then" picture. Do not use words that describe physical characteristics. Use words that describe how you and your loved ones feel. Then write three feeling words to describe yourself, your mother, and your father in the "now" picture.

    (*Note:* If any student has lost a parent, do not have the students describe their parents in the "now" picture.)

- Show the students the picture you have drawn of your family. Then have each student share his/her picture with the group.

- Have the students put their pictures in their folders. Collect the folders.

SESSION 4
GRIEF AND LOSS

Purpose:

To encourage students to identify feelings related to loss and relate those feelings to colors

Materials Required:

For the leader:
- ☐ *Group Opening* (page 9)
- ☐ *Group Rules* (page 10)
- ☐ Materials for *Energizer 14* (page 34)

For each student:
- ☐ Student's folder
- ☐ *Colors Of My Heart* (page 158)
- ☐ Crayons or markers

Preparation:

Read the instructions for *Energizer 14*. Gather the necessary materials.

Make a copy of *Colors Of My Heart* for each student.

Session Content:

- Give each student his/her folder.

- Select a student to read the *Group Opening*.

- Pass the *Group Rules* around. Have each student read one rule aloud until all of the rules have been read.

- Present *Energizer 14*.

- Give each student a copy of *Colors Of My Heart* and crayons or markers. Then say:

    Think back to the time of your loss. Remember how you felt. Choose four or five colors to represent those feelings, then color your heart to reflect the ways you felt.

    At the bottom of the activity sheet, list the names of the colors you chose. Next to each color, write the feeling it represents.

- Have each student share his/her drawing with the group, naming the feeling that each color represents. Then ask:

    Did someone choose to represent loss with a color that you wouldn't associate with loss?

- Note the similarities and differences in the students' choices. Let the students know that there are no right or wrong choices. What matters is that their choices are meaningful to them.

- Have the students put their activity sheets in their folders. Collect the folders.

COLORS OF MY HEART

_____   _____
_____   _____
_____   _____
_____   _____

SESSION 5
GRIEF AND LOSS

Purpose:

To encourage the students to examine their feelings about the loss they have experienced

Materials Required:

For the leader:
- ☐ *Group Opening* (page 9)
- ☐ *Group Rules* (page 10)
- ☐ *Energizer 9* (page 31)

For each student:
- ☐ Student's folder
- ☐ *Incomplete Sentences For Loss* (page 160)
- ☐ Pencil

Preparation:

Read the instructions for *Energizer 9*.

Make a copy of *Incomplete Sentences For Loss* for each student.

Session Content:

- Give each student his/her folder.

- Select a student to read the *Group Opening*.

- Pass the *Group Rules* around. Have each student read one rule aloud until all of the rules have been read.

- Present *Energizer 9*.

- Give each student a copy of *Incomplete Sentences For Loss* and a pencil. Tell the students to complete the activity sheet. Then have the students take turns sharing their responses.

- Have the students put their activity sheets in their folders. Collect the folders.

INCOMPLETE SENTENCES FOR LOSS

Directions: Complete each sentence while thinking about your loss.

If only _____

_____.

I am sorry that _____

_____.

I am glad that _____

_____.

I often feel _____

_____.

Sometimes I am afraid _____

_____.

What bothers me most is _____

_____.

If I could have one wish, it would be _____

_____.

Things would be better if _____

_____.

I can't understand why _____

_____.

What hurts me is _____

_____.

I often worry about _____

_____.

If I could have one more day with the person I lost, I would _____

_____.

The happiest time I had with the person I lost was _____

_____.

The future _____

_____.

SESSION 6
GRIEF AND LOSS

Purpose:

To examine changes that have taken place in the students' families since the loss occurred

Materials Required:

For the leader:
- ☐ *Group Opening* (page 9)
- ☐ *Group Rules* (page 10)
- ☐ Materials for *Energizer 6* (page 25)

For each student:
- ☐ Student's folder
- ☐ *Family Changes* (page 162)
- ☐ Pencil

Preparation:

Read the instructions for *Energizer 6*. Gather and prepare the necessary materials.

Make a copy of *Family Changes* for each student.

Session Content:

- Give each student his/her folder.

- Select a student to read the *Group Opening*.

- Pass the *Group Rules* around. Have each student read one rule aloud until all of the rules have been read.

- Present *Energizer 6*.

- Give each student a copy of *Family Changes* and a pencil. Have the students list the changes that have occurred in their families since the loss. If one of the boxes on the activity sheet pertains to the person lost, tell the students to omit that response. Have the students share their responses with the group.

- Ask the students to bring something of their loved one's to share with the group at the next session. It could be a picture, a piece a jewelry, or any memento that reminds them of their loved one.

- Have the students put their activity sheets in their folders. Collect the folders.

FAMILY CHANGES

Directions: In each box, list the changes that have occurred since the loss of your loved one.

MYSELF

BROTHER(S)

FAMILY

SISTER(S)

MOM

GRANDPARENT(S)

DAD

FRIENDS

CHANGES THAT I LIKE

CHANGES THAT I DON'T LIKE

SESSION 7
GRIEF AND LOSS

Purpose:

To encourage the students to reminisce about their loved one

Materials Required:

For the leader:
- ☐ *Group Opening* (page 9)
- ☐ *Group Rules* (page 10)

For each student:
- ☐ Student's folder
- ☐ Memento of a loved one
- ☐ *Memories* (page 164)
- ☐ Pencil

Preparation:

Make a copy of *Memories* for each student.

Session Content:

- Give each student his/her folder.

- Select a student to read the *Group Opening*.

- Pass the *Group Rules* around. Have each student read one rule aloud until all of the rules have been read.

- Introduce the energizer by saying:

  In the last session, I asked each of you to bring in something of your loved one's to share with the group. For today's energizer, you will take turns sharing your memento.

  Have each student talk about his/her memento and why it is special to him/her.

- Tell the students:

  When you lose someone, you may feel an emptiness inside. It is helpful to fill that emptiness with memories of your loved one.

- Give each student a copy of *Memories* and a pencil. Tell the students to complete the activity sheet. Then have each person share what he/she wrote.

- Have the students put their activity sheets in their folders. Collect the folders.

MEMORIES

Directions: Thinking of your loved one, answer each of the following:

My favorite memories: _____
_____
_____
_____
_____
_____

Something that I am glad that I got to do with my loved one:
_____
_____

A favorite story about my loved one: _____
_____
_____
_____
_____

Something that makes me smile when I think of my loved one:
_____
_____

Something I have that reminds me of my loved one: _____
_____

SESSION 8
GRIEF AND LOSS

Purpose

To have the students make a collage that represents their loved one

Materials Required:

For the leader:
- ☐ *Group Opening* (page 9)
- ☐ *Group Rules* (page 10)
- ☐ Materials for *Energizer 7* (page 30)
- ☐ Selection of catalogs and magazines that can be cut apart

For each student:
- ☐ Scissors
- ☐ Glue
- ☐ Piece of construction paper

Preparation:

Read the instructions for *Energizer 7*. Gather and prepare the necessary materials.

Session Content:

- Select a student to read the *Group Opening*.

- Pass the *Group Rules* around. Have each student read one rule aloud until all of the rules have been read.

- Present *Energizer 7*.

- Give each student a piece of construction paper, scissors, and glue. Then say:

    Today, you are going to make a collage that reminds you of your loved one. It may include your loved one's favorite color, foods, hobbies, and whatever else you want to remember about him or her. You may look through these catalogs and magazines, cut out whatever you need for your collage, and glue the selected pictures onto the construction paper.

- Conclude the lesson by having the students share their collages with the group.

- If a laminator is available, collect the collages and laminate them before the next session. At the next session, give the collages to the students to take home. If a laminator is not available, let the students take their collages with them at the end of today's session.

SESSION 9
GRIEF AND LOSS

Purpose:

To help the students learn about the stages of grief and briefly discuss their loved one's funeral or memorial service

Materials Required:

For the leader:
- ☐ *Group Opening* (page 9)
- ☐ *Group Rules* (page 10)
- ☐ *Energizer 13* (page 33)
- ☐ Chalkboard and chalk or dry-erase board and marker

For each student:
- ☐ Student's folder
- ☐ *The Funeral* (page 168)
- ☐ Pencil

Preparation:

Read the instructions for *Energizer 13*.

Make a copy of *The Funeral* for each student.

Session Content:

- Give each student his/her folder.

- Select a student to read the *Group Opening*.

- Pass the *Group Rules* around. Have each student read one rule aloud until all of the rules have been read.

- Present *Energizer 13*.

- Go to the board and draw two lines. Make one line straight and make the other jagged. Then say:

    There is no set time in which a person heals after losing a loved one.

    Draw a straight line like the one below.

    ☹————————————☺

    Then say:

    You don't go in a straight line from feeling sad to feeling happy again.

    The healing process is more like a jagged line.

    Draw a jagged line like the one below.

    Then say:

    There will be days when you will feel down and sad. On other days, you will feel fine and happy. You will have your ups and downs and even go backward sometimes. This behavior will last for a period of time. It is normal.

- Explain that some people think that people who experience loss go through three stages:

    1. Shock and/or disbelief
    2. Anger and/or depression
    3. Acceptance and moving on

Explain each stage to the students. Ask the students if they see themselves as going through any of these stages. Discuss their responses. Then say:

> *Most people seem to experience these stages. How long you stay in stages one or two is different for each person.*

- Give each student a copy of The Funeral and a pencil. Explain that the next topic the group will discuss is the funeral/memorial service of their loved one. Tell the students to complete the activity sheet. Then have the students share their responses.

(Note: Before presenting this activity, be sure each group member's loved one had a funeral or memorial service. If the loved one of any member of the group did not have a funeral or memorial service, skip this activity.)

Ask the students:

> *Is there anything else you would like to say about your loved one's funeral or memorial service?*

- Have the students put their activity sheets in their folders. Collect the folders.

THE FUNERAL

Directions: People choose to pay their last respects to loved ones in different ways. Some have a traditional funeral, others a memorial service. Some have a public service, others have a private service. As you complete this activity sheet, think about the type of service your loved one had.

I remember _____
_____ .

I remember _____
_____ .

I remember _____
_____ .

My mom/dad _____
_____ .

Something that made me feel good was _____
_____ .

Something that made me feel hurt or angry was _____
_____ .

My final wish for my loved one is _____
_____ .

SESSION 10
GRIEF AND LOSS

Purpose:

To help the students deal with the loss of a loved one during a holiday season

Materials Required:

For the leader:
- ☐ *Group Opening* (page 9)
- ☐ *Group Rules* (page 10)
- ☐ *Energizer 15* (page 34)

For each student:
- ☐ Student's folder
- ☐ *Making Memories* (page 170)
- ☐ Pencil

Preparation:

Read the instructions for *Energizer 15*.

Make a copy of *Making Memories* for each student.

Session Content:

- Give each student his/her folder.

- Select a student to read the *Group Opening*.

- Pass the *Group Rules* around. Have each student read one rule aloud until all of the rules have been read.

- Present *Energizer 15*.

- Tell the students:

    Celebrating holidays can be very difficult after you have lost a loved one. During this time, it is nice to do something or make something special in memory of your loved one.

- Brainstorm about how to remember a loved one during holidays. Some examples could be: making a book of pictures, decorating and lighting a candle, framing a picture of a loved one and giving it as a gift, or making an ornament in memory of your loved one.

- Give each student a copy of *Making Memories* and a pencil. Have the students write the name of the upcoming holiday and complete the activity sheet. Then have the students take turns sharing their thoughts.

- Have the students place their activity sheet in their folders. Collect the folders.

- (*Note:* If a holiday season is approaching and you feel it is appropriate, you may wish to write a letter like the one below and give it and a candle to any student who has lost a loved one.)

Date_____

Dear _____ ,

It is my wish at this _____ season that you light this candle in memory of your _____ . The candle represents *grief*, which is the pain of losing your _____ . It also represents *courage*, which is confronting your sorrow and being able to reach out for comfort. And it stands for memories—which are the times you laughed, the times you cried, the times you both were angry, the silly things you did together, and the caring and joy that you gave each other. Lastly, it represents the lights of _____ love. During this season, let the light of this candle shine in memory of your _____ .

Sincerely,

MAKING MEMORIES

Upcoming holiday _____

My best memory of my _____ is
_____
_____ .

It will be different this year because _____
_____
_____

Some things will still be the same. They are _____
_____
_____ .

I will celebrate the memory of my loved one this holiday by
_____
_____

SESSION 11
GRIEF AND LOSS

Purpose:

To review what has been presented in previous lessons

Materials Required:

For the leader:
- ☐ *Group Opening* (page 9)
- ☐ *Group Rules* (page 10)
- ☐ *Energizer 16* (page 35)
- ☐ *Bingo Numbers* (pages 42-43)
- ☐ Container

For each student:
- ☐ Student's folder
- ☐ *Grief Bingo* (page 173)
- ☐ Markers or pens of two different-color inks

Preparation:

Read the instructions for *Energizer 16*.

Make a copy of *Grief Bingo* for each student.

Make a copy of the *Bingo Numbers*. Cut the numbers apart and place them in the container.

Session Content:

- Give each student his/her folder.

- Select a student to read the *Group Opening*.

- Pass the *Group Rules* around. Have each student read one rule aloud until all of the rules have been read.

- Present *Energizer 16*.

- Tell the students:

    We are going to play Grief Bingo. *As we play this game, we will review things we have learned in the past few weeks.*

- Give each student a copy of *Grief Bingo* and markers or pens of two different-color inks. Explain how the students should fill in their bingo cards by saying:

    The letters G R I E F are printed at the top of the columns. Below each letter is a number range. Using one color of ink/marker, fill in each circle in each column with one of the numbers within the indicated range. For example, you may choose 3, 5, 8, 12, and 15 to fill in the circles in the column under the letter G.

- Explain how the game is played by saying:

    I will draw one number at a time from this container. As I draw each number, look at your Grief Bingo *card to see if you have written that number on your card. If you have that number on your card, raise your hand. I will call on you to complete the sentence written in that space. You may then place an X in the box using the other color of ink/marker. The first person to get five X's in a row should call out* Grief Bingo! *He or she will win the game.*

- Play the game.

- Discuss the statements on the *Grief Bingo* cards. Ask the students which were easy to complete and which were difficult.

- Have the students put their bingo cards in their folders. Collect the folders.

G R I E F

BINGO

G #1–#15	R #16–#30	I #31–#45	E #46–#60	F #61–#75
Someone I loved and have lost is …	A color that represents my feeling of loss is …	A good time I had with my loved one was …	If only …	If I could spend one more day with my loved one, I would …
Some feelings I had when I lost my loved one were …	I can accept …	A funny thing that happened with my loved one was …	I am sorry that …	The memento I shared with the group was …
The hardest thing about losing someone is …	I cannot accept …	FREE SPACE BINGO	Sometimes I am afraid …	Three stages of grief are …
I'd like to tell the person I lost …	If I could have done things differently …	I wish …	I often worry about …	My favorite memory of my loved one is …
I don't understand …	Three words that describe my loved one are …	I like to talk about my loved one with …	Something that has changed in my family since my loss is …	The future …

GRAB BAG GUIDANCE © 2005 MAR*CO PRODUCTS, INC. 1-800-448-2197

SESSION 12
GRIEF AND LOSS

Purpose:

To bring closure to the group

Materials Required:

For the leader:
- ☐ *Group Opening* (page 9)
- ☐ *Group Rules* (page 10)
- ☐ Materials for *Energizer 10* (page 32)

For each student:
- ☐ Student's folder
- ☐ Paper
- ☐ Pencil

Preparation:

Read the instructions for *Energizer 10*. Gather the necessary materials.

Session Content:

- Give each student his/her folder.

- Select a student to read the *Group Opening*.

- Pass the *Group Rules* around. Have each student read one rule aloud until all of the rules have been read.

- Present *Energizer 10*.

- Give each student paper and a pencil. Ask the students to write a letter to their loved one. Tell the students to write what they would like to say to their loved one if they could see him/her one more time. Have the students share their letters with the group.

- Thank the students for taking part in the group, especially for sharing with others a truly personal part of themselves and their lives. Tell the students it is your hope that through their participation in the activities it will be easier for them to cope with and accept what has happened and move forward.

- Have the students go through their folders and give you any papers they want shredded. They may keep their folders and any papers they want.

- To conclude the group, have the students participate in the *Jelly Roll Squeeze* activity. Have the students stand side by side with their arms around each other's waists. Beginning on one end, tell the students to start to roll toward the other end. The first person should roll toward the second person, the second person should roll toward the third person, the third toward the fourth, on so on. When everyone is curled in, say, "Squeeze" on the count of three.

SELF-ESTEEM

SESSION 1
SELF-ESTEEM

Purpose:

To introduce the group members to each other, explain the purpose of the group, and emphasize the importance of good listening skills

Materials Required:

For the leader:
- ☐ *Group Opening* (page 9)
- ☐ *Group Rules* (page 10)
- ☐ Materials for *Energizer 1* (page 13)
- ☐ Materials for *Energizer 2* (page 14)

For each student:
- ☐ 2-pocket manila folder
- ☐ Crayons or markers
- ☐ Pencil

Preparation:

If you have not already done so, reproduce the *Group Rules* and *Group Opening*. Laminate the pages if possible.

Read the instructions for *Energizer 1* and *Energizer 2*. Gather and prepare the necessary materials.

Session Content:

- Introduce the *Group Rules* and the *Group Opening* to the students.

- Explain that the purpose of the group is to discuss *self-esteem* and the importance of this subject to them.

- Present *Energizer 1*.

- Give each student a folder, crayons or markers, and a pencil. Tell the students the folders will be used to hold their handouts.

- Instruct the students to write their name on the folder, along with the day and class period the group meets. Allow time for the students to use the crayons or markers to decorate their folders.

- Present *Energizer 2* to reinforce the concept that listening to each other while participating in group sessions is very important.

- Collect the folders. (*Note:* The folders will be collected by the leader at the end of each session. At the final session, the students may keep whatever they want from their folders. Shred anything the students do not want to keep.)

SESSION 2
SELF-ESTEEM

Purpose:

To help the students relate feelings they have experienced and visualize their family structure through an art activity

Materials Required:

For the leader:
- ☐ *Group Opening* (page 9)
- ☐ *Group Rules* (page 10)
- ☐ Materials for *Energizer 4* (page 23)
- ☐ Piece of white drawing paper
- ☐ Colored pencils or markers
- ☐ Pencil

For each student:
- ☐ Student's folder
- ☐ Piece of white drawing paper
- ☐ Pencil
- ☐ Colored pencils or markers

Preparation:

Read the instructions for *Energizer 4*. Gather and prepare the necessary materials.

Following the directions in the session, draw a picture of your family to show the students.

Session Content:

- Give each student his/her folder.

- Select a student to read the *Group Opening*.

- Pass the *Group Rules* around. Have each student read one rule aloud until all of the rules have been read.

- Present *Energizer 4*.

- Give each student a piece of white drawing paper, a pencil, and colored pencils or markers. Show the students the picture you drew of your family. Then say:

    Draw a picture of your family. Draw a circle to represent each family member. In each circle, write the initials of the person it represents. If you believe family members have a close relationship, draw their circles close to each other. If you believe family members do not have a close relationship, draw their circles farther apart. At the bottom of the paper, write three words that describe your mother, your father, and yourself.

  Tell the students how much time they have to complete the activity. When the allotted time has elapsed, have each student talk about his/her family picture.

- Have the students place their pictures in their folders. Collect the folders.

SESSION 3
SELF-ESTEEM

Purpose:

To encourage the students to examine their own qualities and the qualities of people they admire

Materials Required:

For the leader:
- ☐ *Group Opening* (page 9)
- ☐ *Group Rules* (page 10)
- ☐ *Energizer 9* (page 31)

For each student:
- ☐ Student's folder
- ☐ *My Personal Car* (page 179)
- ☐ *Whom Do You Admire?* (page 180)
- ☐ Pencil

Preparation:

Read the instructions for *Energizer 9*.

Make a copy of *My Personal Car* and *Whom Do You Admire?* for each student.

Session Content:

- Give each student his/her folder.

- Select a student to read the *Group Opening*.

- Pass the *Group Rules* around. Have each student read one rule aloud until all of the rules have been read.

- Present *Energizer 9*.

- Give each student a copy of *My Personal Car*, a copy of *Whom Do You Admire?*, and a pencil. Have the students complete *My Personal Car* by following the directions on the activity sheet. Then have the students share their answers with the group.

- Ask the students to explain the meaning of the word *admire*. (Answers should include *someone you respect, look up to, etc.*) Have the students complete *Whom Do You Admire?* Then have the students tell the group whom they admire and why.

- Have the students place their activity sheets in their folders. Collect the folders.

MY PERSONAL CAR

Directions: Design your personal sports car with information about yourself.

- On the hood of the car, write the qualities of being a good friend that you possess.
- On the door, write something you would like others to say about you.
- On one wheel, write your best quality.
- On the other wheel, write a kind thing that you have done.
- On the trunk, write about a time you helped someone out.
- On the roof, write your dream.

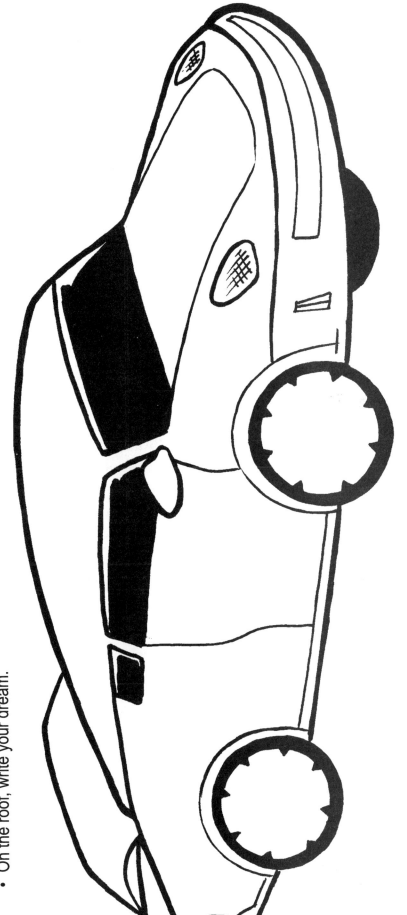

WHOM DO YOU ADMIRE?

Whom do you admire? _____

Why do you admire this person? _____
_____
_____
_____
_____

What qualities does this person possess? _____
_____
_____
_____
_____

☆☆☆☆☆

Look at yourself.
Chances are, you have many of the same qualities
as the person you admire.

What are those qualities? _____
_____
_____
_____
_____

SESSION 4
SELF-ESTEEM

Purpose:

To encourage the students to ignore negativity and develop their own self-talk statements

Materials Required:

For the leader:
- ☐ *Group Opening* (page 9)
- ☐ *Group Rules* (page 10)
- ☐ Materials for *Energizer 5* (page 24)

For each student:
- ☐ Student's folder
- ☐ *Positive Mirror* (page 182)
- ☐ Pencil

Preparation:

Read the instructions for *Energizer 5*. Gather and prepare the necessary materials.

Make a copy of *Positive Mirror* for each student.

Session Content:

- Give each student his/her folder.

- Select a student to read the *Group Opening*.

- Pass the *Group Rules* around. Have each student read one rule aloud until all of the rules have been read.

- Present *Energizer 5*.

- Tell the students:

You have the power to enhance your own self-esteem! If someone says something negative to you, you have the choice to feel hurt or mad. Or you can ignore the comment and not let what was said affect you. It is important not to let another person's negative comments lower your self-esteem. To raise your self-esteem, try to forget about what was said and get on with your life. Just let negative comments "bounce off" of you.

Self-esteem comes from within, but it does not always come easily. Building up your self-esteem takes practice. One method of building up self-esteem is self-talk. Self-talk is saying or thinking positive things about yourself. For example:

"I am the best that I can be."

"A few bad moments don't have to ruin my day."

- Give each student a copy of *Positive Mirror* and a pencil. Have the students write some positive statements they can tell themselves when they need to use self-talk. Then ask the students to share their self-talk statements by taking turns and reading one statement at a time. Continue going around the group until every self-talk statement has been read aloud.

- Have the students place their activity sheets in their folders. Collect the folders.

POSITIVE MIRROR

Directions: Write some positive statements that you can make to yourself to enhance your self-esteem.

BE YOUR #1 FAN!

SESSION 5
SELF-ESTEEM

Purpose:

To help students understand that, depending upon how they react to a situation, they may have control over its outcome

Materials Required:

For the leader:
- ☐ *Group Opening* (page 9)
- ☐ *Group Rules* (page 10)
- ☐ Materials for *Energizer 3* (page 22)
- ☐ Chalkboard and chalk or dry-erase board and marker

For each student:
- ☐ Student's folder
- ☐ *About Me* (page 185)
- ☐ Pencil

Preparation:

Read the instructions for *Energizer 3*. Gather the necessary materials.

Make a copy of *About Me* for each student.

Session Content:

- Give each student his/her folder.

- Select a student to read the *Group Opening*.

- Pass the *Group Rules* around. Have each student read one rule aloud until all of the rules have been read.

- Present *Energizer 3*.

- Tell the students:

    Self-esteem is how you feel about yourself. You have the power to enhance your self-esteem by changing how you feel about yourself.

- Go to the board and write the following formula:

    S   (Situation)
    + R (Reaction or Response)
    ─────────────
    = O (Outcome)

- Then say:

    How you react or respond to a situation will "equal" or affect the outcome. If you do not like the outcome, you must change how you respond to similar situations to get different outcomes.

    *For example: If the **situation** is homework and your **response** is to not do it, **what is the outcome?** (Pause for student responses. The students will give various answers such as failure, possible detention, and being grounded.)*

- Have the students use the same example and change the response. For example: If the **situation** is homework and your **response** is to do it, **what is the outcome?** *(Better grades, privileges, etc.)* Emphasize that by changing our reaction or response to a situation, we can often achieve the outcome we want.

- Remind the students about the *self-talk* concept introduced in the previous lesson. Explain that by replacing negative thoughts about themselves with positive thoughts, they can enhance their self-esteem. Give the students the following example:

    If someone says something negative to you, you can say, "Cancel" in your mind. Do not let negative thoughts enter your head. You may also say, "I'm not perfect, but I am the best I can be."

  Have the students give examples of other positive thoughts. Write their ideas on the board.

- Remind the students:

    Do not compare yourself to others, because doing so often results in low self-esteem. People can always find something about another person they wish they possessed themselves. Be happy with the person you are. Chances are, other people see something about you that they wish they had.

- Give each student a copy of *About Me* and a pencil. Have the students complete the open-ended sentences, then share their answers with the group.

- Conclude the session by telling the students to remember that positive thoughts enhance self-esteem and negative thoughts damage self-esteem. Think positive!

- Have the students place their activity sheets in their folders. Collect the folders.

ABOUT ME

Directions: Complete the following sentences about yourself.

I wish _____
_____.

Something that I have done to help others is _____
_____.

Someone I respect is _____.

Something I am good at is_____.

Something I value is _____.

Someone I value is _____.

A contribution that I would like to make to society is ____
_____.

Something you may not know about me is _____
_____.

SESSION 6
SELF-ESTEEM

Purpose:

To encourage the students to evaluate their strengths and weaknesses and review ways to raise their self-esteem

Materials Required:

For the leader:
- ☐ *Group Opening* (page 9)
- ☐ *Group Rules* (page 10)
- ☐ Materials for *Energizer 6* (page 25)

For each student:
- ☐ Student's folder
- ☐ *How Well Do You Know Yourself?* (page 187)
- ☐ Pencil

Preparation:

Read the instructions for *Energizer 6*. Gather and prepare the necessary materials.

Make a copy of *How Well Do You Know Yourself?* for each student.

Session Content:

- Give each student his/her folder.

- Select a student to read the *Group Opening*.

- Pass the *Group Rules* around. Have each student read one rule aloud until all of the rules have been read.

- Present *Energizer 6*.

- Give each student a copy of *How Well Do You Know Yourself?* and a pencil. Tell the students to complete the activity sheet according to the directions. Then discuss the traits and the questions at the bottom of the page.

- Discuss the following ways to improve one's self-esteem:

    Accept yourself. Be satisfied with who you are.

    Do things for others. When you help others, you feel good. Treat others the way you would like them to treat you.

    Give yourself a break. Don't be tough on yourself. You are human. You are going to make mistakes, and you can learn from them.

    Enjoy yourself and the world around you.

    Emulate people whom you respect.

    Focus on the positive, not the negative.

    Don't be afraid to take risks. It is okay to fail.

    Let go of past regrets. Let go of your regrets and move on.

- Ask the students to name some additional ways they believe they can raise their self-esteem.

- Have the students place their activity sheets in their folders. Collect the folders.

HOW WELL DO YOU KNOW YOURSELF?

Directions: Rate yourself on the following traits. Number 1 is low, 5 is high, and 3 would be average. Put an ✗ on the line where you think each of your traits belongs.

I AM FAIR	1 . . . . . 2 . . . . . 3 . . . . . 4 5
I AM KIND	1 . . . . . 2 . . . . . 3 . . . . . 4 5
I AM HELPFUL	1 . . . . . 2 . . . . . 3 . . . . . 4 5
I AM CONFIDENT	1 . . . . . 2 . . . . . 3 . . . . . 4 5
I AM A GOOD LISTENER	1 . . . . . 2 . . . . . 3 . . . . . 4 5
I AM ARTISTIC	1 . . . . . 2 . . . . . 3 . . . . . 4 5
I AM ATHLETIC	1 . . . . . 2 . . . . . 3 . . . . . 4 5
I AM GOOD AT ACADEMICS	1 . . . . . 2 . . . . . 3 . . . . . 4 5
I AM DEPENDABLE	1 . . . . . 2 . . . . . 3 . . . . . 4 5
I AM TRUSTWORTHY	1 . . . . . 2 . . . . . 3 . . . . . 4 5
I AM OPEN-MINDED	1 . . . . . 2 . . . . . 3 . . . . . 4 5
I AM ACCEPTING	1 . . . . . 2 . . . . . 3 . . . . . 4 5
I HAVE SENSE OF HUMOR	1 . . . . . 2 . . . . . 3 . . . . . 4 5

Add any traits that you possess that were not mentioned above.

_____	1 . . . . . 2 . . . . . 3 . . . . . 4 5
_____	1 . . . . . 2 . . . . . 3 . . . . . 4 5
_____	1 . . . . . 2 . . . . . 3 . . . . . 4 5
_____	1 . . . . . 2 . . . . . 3 . . . . . 4 5

Look at the qualities you rated highly. Commend yourself for these qualities! Look at the ones you rated lower. Are they important to you? If they are, what can you do to improve them?

Know yourself. Be satisfied with who you are.

SESSION 7
SELF-ESTEEM

Purpose:

To review what has been presented in previous lessons

Materials Required:

For the leader:
- ☐ *Group Opening* (page 9)
- ☐ *Group Rules* (page 10)
- ☐ Materials for *Energizer 17* (page 35)
- ☐ *Bingo Numbers* (pages 42-43)
- ☐ Container

For each student:
- ☐ Student's folder
- ☐ *Self-Worth Bingo* (page 190)
- ☐ Markers or pens of two different-color inks

Preparation

Read the instructions for *Energizer 17*. Gather the necessary materials.

Make a copy of *Self-Worth Bingo* for each student.

Make a copy of the *Bingo Numbers*. Cut the numbers apart and place them in the container.

Session Content:

- Give each student his/her folder.

- Select a student to read the *Group Opening*.

- Pass the *Group Rules* around. Have each student read one rule aloud until all of the rules have been read.

- Present *Energizer 17*.

- Tell the students:

    We are going to play Self-Worth Bingo. *As we play this game, we will review things we have learned in the past few weeks.*

- Give each student a copy of *Self-Worth Bingo* and markers or pens of two different-color inks. Explain how the students should fill in their bingo cards by saying:

    The letters W O R T H *are printed at the top of the columns. Below each letter is a number range. Using one color of ink/marker, fill in each circle in each column with one of the numbers within the indicated range. For example, you may choose 3, 5, 8, 12, and 15 to fill in the circles in the column under the letter* W.

- Explain how the game is played by saying:

    I will draw one number at a time from this container. As I draw each number, look at your Self-Worth Bingo *card to see if you have written that number on your card. If you have that number on your card, raise your hand. I will call*

188 GRAB BAG GUIDANCE © 2005 MAR*CO PRODUCTS, INC. 1-800-448-2197

on you to complete the sentence written in that space. You may then place an X in the box using the other color of ink/marker. The first person to get five X's in a row should call out Self-Worth Bingo! *He or she will win the game.*

- Play the game.

- Discuss the statements on the *Self-Worth Bingo* cards. Ask the students which were easy to complete and which were difficult.

- Have the students put their bingo cards in their folders. Collect the folders.

WORTH

W #1–#15	O #16–#30	R #31–#45	T #46–#60	H #61–#75
Someone whom I admire is …	Something I could teach someone else is …	I would like to compliment (GROUP MEMBER'S NAME) by saying …	If I could spend a day with anyone, it would be …	Something that wears me out is …
One thing I like about my best friend is …	My best trait is …	Something a friend did that helped me out is …	If I had $500.00, I would …	My favorite place is …
My favorite subject is …	Something I can do to raise my self-esteem is …	FREE SPACE BINGO	My idol is …	If I were older, …
A trait I would like to improve is …	I am good at …	Something I would like to do better is …	I helped a friend out by …	If I could be anything I wanted, I would be …
The best thing about my family is …	The best thing about school is …	If I could visit any place in the world, I would go …	Some advice I would give to someone younger is …	I wish …

190 GRAB BAG GUIDANCE © 2005 MAR*CO PRODUCTS, INC. 1-800-448-2197

SESSION 8
SELF-ESTEEM

Purpose:

To encourage the students to express dreams they have had for a long time and explore the possibilities and obstacles to making them come true

Materials Required:

For the leader:
- ☐ *Group Opening* (page 9)
- ☐ *Group Rules* (page 10)
- ☐ Materials for *Energizer 7* (page 30)

For each student:
- ☐ Student's folder
- ☐ *My Dream* (page 192)
- ☐ Pencil

Preparation:

Read the instructions for *Energizer 7*. Gather and prepare the necessary materials.

Make a copy of *My Dream* for each student.

Session Content:

- Give each student his/her folder.

- Select a student to read the *Group Opening*.

- Pass the *Group Rules* around. Have each student read one rule aloud until all of the rules have been read.

- Present *Energizer 7*.

- Give each student a copy of *My Dream* and a pencil. Have the students complete the activity sheet.

Discuss the completed activity sheets in length. **This topic is extremely important to the development of self-esteem.** Students should explore how realistic their dreams may be, what they can do to make their dreams come true, and how to recognize and overcome any obstacles that may stand in their way.

- Have the students place their activity sheets in their folders. Collect the folders.

 # MY DREAM

What is your dream in life? Where are you headed? _____
_____
_____
_____
_____

What can you do to make your dream come true? _____
_____
_____
_____
_____

What are some obstacles that may be in the way? _____
_____
_____
_____

How can you overcome them? _____
_____
_____
_____

 **MOVE TOWARD YOUR DREAM!**
DON'T LET ANYONE DISCOURAGE YOU
FROM MAKING YOUR DREAM COME TRUE.

SESSION 9
SELF-ESTEEM

Purpose:

To have students examine the trait of self-esteem

Materials Required:

For the leader:
- ☐ *Group Opening* (page 9)
- ☐ *Group Rules* (page 10)
- ☐ *Energizer 11* (page 32)
- ☐ Chalkboard and chalk or dry-erase board and marker

For each student:
- ☐ Student's folder
- ☐ Construction paper
- ☐ Marker

Preparation:

Read the instructions for *Energizer 11*.

Session Content:

- Give each student his/her folder.

- Select a student to read the *Group Opening*.

- Pass the *Group Rules* around. Have each student read one rule aloud until all of the rules have been read.

- Present *Energizer 11*.

- Give each student a piece of construction paper and a marker. Have the students make an acrostic using the letters of their name. Next to each letter, they should write a word that describes themselves. Show the students the following example:

    M arvelous
    A wesome
    G irl
    G o-getter
    I nquisitive
    E xcellent

    Have each student share his/her acrostic with the group.

- Write the word *self-esteem* on the board. Have the students make an acrostic using words that might describe someone with high self-esteem.

    S ociable
    E nergetic
    L ovable
    F unny

    E nthusiastic
    S atisfied
    T houghtful
    E xcited
    E xcellent
    M arvelous

- Have the students place their activity sheets in their folders. Collect the folders.

SESSION 10
SELF-ESTEEM

Purpose:

To give encouragement to fellow group members and bring closure to the group

Materials Required:

For the leader:
- ☐ *Group Opening* (page 9)
- ☐ *Group Rules* (page 10)
- ☐ Materials for *Energizer 10* (page 32)

For each student:
- ☐ Student's folder
- ☐ Index cards
- ☐ Pencil

Preparation:

Read the instructions for *Energizer 10*. Gather the necessary materials.

Session Content:

- Give each student his/her folder.

- Select a student to read the *Group Opening*.

- Pass the *Group Rules* around. Have each student read one rule aloud until all of the rules have been read.

- Present *Energizer 10*.

- Give each group member a pencil and as many index cards as there are students in the group, less one. Feature one group member at a time by having the other students write something nice to him/her. Tell the students to begin with "Dear ____." Make sure each student signs his/her name.

  After being featured, each student should have an index card from every other student in the group. Tell the students they may keep the cards and read them if they ever start feeling low. They may want to display the cards in their bedroom and read them often.

- Have the students go through their folders and give you any papers they want shredded. They may keep their folders and any papers they want.

- To conclude the group, have the students participate in the *Jelly Roll Squeeze* activity. Have the students stand side by side with their arms around each other's waists. Beginning on one end, tell the students to start to roll toward the other end. The first person should roll toward the second person, the second person should roll toward the third person, the third toward the fourth, on so on. When everyone is curled in, say, "Squeeze" on the count of three.

- Thank the students for taking part in the group, especially for sharing with others. Remind them to think positively and enhance their own self-esteem.

Skills for Success

SESSION 1
SKILLS FOR SUCCESS

Purpose:

To introduce the group members to each other, explain the purpose of the group, and emphasize the importance of good listening skills

Materials Required:

For the leader:
- ☐ *Group Opening* (page 9)
- ☐ *Group Rules* (page 10)
- ☐ Materials for *Energizer 1* (page 13)
- ☐ Materials for *Energizer 2* (page 14)

For each student:
- ☐ 2-pocket manila folder
- ☐ Crayons or markers
- ☐ Pencil

Preparation:

If you have not already done so, reproduce the *Group Rules* and *Group Opening*. Laminate the pages if possible.

Read the instructions for *Energizer 1* and *Energizer 2*. Gather and prepare the necessary materials.

Session Content:

- Introduce the *Group Rules* and the *Group Opening* to the students.

- Present *Energizer 1*.

- Give each student a folder, crayons or markers, and a pencil. Tell the students the folders will be used to hold their handouts.

- Instruct the students to write their name on the folder, along with the day and class period the group meets. Allow time for the students to use the crayons or markers to decorate their folders.

- Present *Energizer 2* to reinforce the concept that listening to each other while participating in group sessions is very important.

- Tell the students that each of them has a lot of ability. The purpose of this group is to give them some tips on how to use their abilities successfully, with the hope they will apply the skills learned in this group to their everyday lives.

- Collect the folders. (*Note:* The folders will be collected by the leader at the end of each session. At the final session, the students may keep whatever they want from their folders. Shred anything the students do not want to keep.)

SESSION 2
SKILLS FOR SUCCESS

Purpose:

To correlate positive character traits with success

Materials Required:

For the leader:
- ☐ *Group Opening* (page 9)
- ☐ *Group Rules* (page 10)
- ☐ Materials for *Energizer 5* (page 24)

For each student:
- ☐ Student's folder
- ☐ *Success* (page 198)
- ☐ Pencil

Preparation:

Read the instructions for *Energizer 5*. Gather and prepare the necessary materials.

Make a copy of *Success* for each student.

Session Content:

- Give each student his/her folder.

- Select a student to read the *Group Opening*.

- Pass the *Group Rules* around. Have each student read one rule aloud until all of the rules have been read.

- Present *Energizer 5*.

- Give each student a copy of *Success* and a pencil. Tell the students to read the directions and complete the activity sheet.

- Discuss the relationship of positive traits to success. Introduce the topic by giving the students the following logical analogy:

    If a responsible person works hard,

    and hard work leads to success,

    then successful people are responsible.

  Have the students discuss the analogy and make up other analogies that will emphasize the fact that success is related to positive character traits.

- Review each trait listed on the activity sheet. Discuss how each trait relates to success in school, with friends, and/or in a job.

- Have the students place their activity sheets in their folders. Collect the folders.

SUCCESS

Directions: Success in school, with friends, and in a job relates to positive traits you possess. Read the traits listed below, think about how successful you are in each of them. Then rate yourself. Number 1 is low, 5 is high, and 3 would be average. Put an **X** on the line where you think the trait of yours belongs.

FAIRNESS	1 . . . . 2 . . . . 3 . . . . 4 5
RESPECTFULNESS	1 . . . . 2 . . . . 3 . . . . 4 5
HELPFULNESS	1 . . . . 2 . . . . 3 . . . . 4 5
CONFIDENCE	1 . . . . 2 . . . . 3 . . . . 4 5
LISTENING	1 . . . . 2 . . . . 3 . . . . 4 5
RESPONSIBILITY	1 . . . . 2 . . . . 3 . . . . 4 5
PROMPTNESS	1 . . . . 2 . . . . 3 . . . . 4 5
ACADEMICS	1 . . . . 2 . . . . 3 . . . . 4 5
CONSCIENTIOUS	1 . . . . 2 . . . . 3 . . . . 4 5
TRUSTWORTHINESS	1 . . . . 2 . . . . 3 . . . . 4 5
OPEN-MINDEDNESS	1 . . . . 2 . . . . 3 . . . . 4 5
ACCEPTANCE OF MISTAKES	1 . . . . 2 . . . . 3 . . . . 4 5
SENSE OF HUMOR	1 . . . . 2 . . . . 3 . . . . 4 5

Look at the traits you rated highest and commend yourself for them! Look at the traits you rated lower. The skills you will learn in this group may help you raise these scores.

SESSION 3
SKILLS FOR SUCCESS

Purpose:

To relate *decision-making* to *success*

Materials Required:

For the leader:
- ☐ *Group Opening* (page 9)
- ☐ *Group Rules* (page 10)
- ☐ *Energizer 12* (page 33)

For each student:
- ☐ Student's folder
- ☐ *5 C's In Decision-Making* (page 201)

For each pair of students:
- ☐ *Decision-Making* (page 202)
- ☐ Pencil

Preparation:

Read the instructions for *Energizer 12*.

Make a copy of *5 C's In Decision-Making* for each student.

Make a copy of *Decision-Making* for each pair of students.

Session Content:

- Give each student his/her folder.

- Select a student to read the *Group Opening*.

- Pass the *Group Rules* around. Have each student read one rule aloud until all of the rules have been read.

- Present *Energizer 12*.

- Tell the students:

    Decisions you make are either automatic, such as brushing your teeth; daily, such as deciding what to wear; or major, such as deciding where to go to work or to college.

    Every decision you make says something about who you are and determines whether you will be successful. For example: If you decide not to brush your teeth every day, that decision could lead to dental problems and mean that you will have not successfully taken care of your body.

    Ask the students:

    How could choosing the wrong college affect success? (You might pick a school that doesn't fit your needs, doesn't offer the program you want to study, etc.)

- Give each student a copy of *5 C's In Decision-Making*. Explain the activity sheet by saying:

    Suppose you had to decide whether to try out for the soccer team or join chorus. To do this, you should use the 5 C's In Decision-Making*:*

    1. **Clarify:**
       Decide if you want to try out for the soccer team or join chorus.

2. **Consider The Choices:**
   Try out for the soccer team or join chorus.

3. **Compare and Weigh:**
   Pros for soccer: I'll get exercise; kids will look up to me.
   Cons for soccer: I'm not a very good athlete; I might not make the team.
   Pros for chorus: I'll get to sing in concerts; I enjoy music.
   Cons for chorus: My friends are not in chorus.

4. **Choose The Best Option:**
   (Ask the students what the best choice would be.)

5. **Carry Out Your Plan**

Then say:

After making a decision, it is good to evaluate your choice and the outcome of your decision. Evaluating decisions can help you make wise choices and avoid making the same mistakes in similar situations.

- Divide the students into pairs. Give each pair of students a copy of *Decision-Making* and a pencil. Have the students read the description of each situation, then decide, with their partner, what the best decision for each one would be. Then have each pair of students share its answers, explaining to the group how they arrived at each decision.

- Have the students place the *5 C's In Decision-Making* in their folders. Have the students decide which member of each pair will put the *Decision-Making* activity sheet in his/her folder. Collect the folders.

5 C's IN DECISION-MAKING

1
Clarify or define the decision.
Ask yourself: what, where, how, when, why, and whom.

2
Consider the choices.
Look at all the alternatives.

3
Compare and weigh.
Look at all angles, analyze, prioritize.

4
Choose the best option.

5
Carry out your plan.

After making a decision, it is good to evaluate your choice and the outcome of your decision. Evaluating your decisions can help you make wise choices and avoid making the same mistakes over and over again.

DECISION-MAKING

Directions: With your partner, use the *5 C's In Decision-Making* to make a decision about each of the following four situations.

Peer Pressure
Your friends want you to go to the mall after school. You have a major project due tomorrow in social studies class and need the time to complete it. What will you decide to do?

_____
_____
_____
_____

Home
Your mom told you that if you get your chores done on Saturday, you may go with your friends to the movies Saturday night. On Saturday morning, your friends call and say they have to go to the matinee. You can't finish your chores that soon. What will you decide to do?

_____
_____
_____
_____

School
Your math grade has dropped. You have an opportunity to do an extra-credit assignment to bring it up, but doing the assignment means giving up your free time, which you don't want to do. What will you decide to do?

_____
_____
_____
_____

Friends
You heard that your best friend was talking about you. You feel betrayed and are thinking about ending the friendship. What will you decide to do?

_____
_____
_____
_____

SESSION 4
SKILLS FOR SUCCESS

Purpose:

To examine the reasons people fail and to learn to change negative beliefs into positive beliefs

Materials Required:

For the leader:
- ☐ *Group Opening* (page 9)
- ☐ *Group Rules* (page 10)
- ☐ Materials for *Energizer 4* (page 23)
- ☐ Chart paper
- ☐ Marker
- ☐ Masking tape

For each student:
- ☐ Student's folder
- ☐ Sticky notes
- ☐ *Changing Negative Beliefs Into Positive Beliefs* (page 204)
- ☐ Pencil

Preparation:

Read the instructions for *Energizer 4*. Gather and prepare the necessary materials.

Title a piece of chart paper *Reasons Why People Fail*. Hang the chart on the wall.

Make a copy of *Changing Negative Beliefs Into Positive Beliefs* for each student.

Session Content:

- Give each student his/her folder.

- Select a student to read the *Group Opening*.

- Pass the *Group Rules* around. Have each student read one rule aloud until all of the rules have been read.

- Present *Energizer 4*.

- Give each student sticky notes and a pencil. On the notes, have the students write all the reasons they can think of why people do not succeed. Then tell the students to post their notes on the *Reasons Why People Fail* chart. Discuss what the students wrote.

- Continue the session by saying:

   We limit ourselves! Many students believe they can't achieve something because they tell themselves they can't. In order to be successful, it is important that you know: You, and only you, can change how you think about things. You have the power to change how you look at things, how you approach things, and what you believe. You can do this through self-talk. Self-talk can change negative beliefs into positive beliefs. A negative belief would be: "I am bad at playing soccer." A positive believe would be: "If I practice, I will get better at soccer."

- Give each student a copy of *Changing Negative Beliefs To Positive Beliefs*. Have the students complete the activity sheet, then share their answers with the group.

- Have the students place their activity sheets in their folders. Collect the folders.

CHANGING NEGATIVE BELIEFS INTO POSITIVE BELIEFS

Directions: Change each of the negative belief statements into a positive belief statement.

NEGATIVE ⇨ ⇨ ⇨   **POSITIVE**
I can't do this work.
_____
_____

NEGATIVE ⇨ ⇨ ⇨   **POSITIVE**
I am stupid.
_____
_____

NEGATIVE ⇨ ⇨ ⇨   **POSITIVE**
I don't care.
_____
_____

NEGATIVE ⇨ ⇨ ⇨   **POSITIVE**
It doesn't matter.
_____
_____

NEGATIVE ⇨ ⇨ ⇨   **POSITIVE**
I can't do anything right.
_____
_____

Focus on positive thoughts.
Build yourself "up" instead of tearing yourself "down."

SESSION 5
SKILLS FOR SUCCESS

Purpose:

To introduce the importance of goal-setting

Materials Required:

For the leader:
- ☐ *Group Opening* (page 9)
- ☐ *Group Rules* (page 10)
- ☐ *Energizer 11* (page 32)

For each student:
- ☐ Student's folder
- ☐ *Traits I Possess* (page 206)
- ☐ *Goals* (page 207)
- ☐ Pencil

Preparation:

Read the instructions for *Energizer 11*.

Make a copy of *Traits I Possess* and *Goals* for each student.

Session Content:

- Give each student his/her folder.

- Select a student to read the *Group Opening*.

- Pass the *Group Rules* around. Have each student read one rule aloud until all of the rules have been read.

- Present *Energizer 11*.

- Give each student a copy of *Traits I Possess* and a pencil. Have the students complete the activity sheet, then discuss their choices.

- Tell the students:

    Goal-setting is important in many ways. It helps you improve upon your strengths and strengthen your weaknesses. Setting goals can also provide direction. Keep in mind: Aim for excellence, not perfection. Goal-setting can help you achieve success.

- Give each student a copy of *Goals*. Discuss each letter and what is written after it:

    Give yourself direction. *How? Think about where you are headed, so you can make decisions about how to get there.*

    Organize and prioritize your goals. *Why? This will determine where you are and where you are headed.*

    Always make realistic and attainable goals. *Why? If you don't, you could easily get discouraged and give up.*

    List obstacles that may get in the way. *Why? Be aware, so that you can prevent interference.*

    Set more goals once you reach your goal. *Why? So you keep improving.*

- Tell the students that the group will continue to work on goal-setting at the next session.

- Have the students place their activity sheets in their folders. Collect the folders.

TRAITS I POSSESS

Directions: Put a check mark (✔) next to every trait you possess. You may add more of your own traits at the bottom of the page.

- ☐ HELPFUL
- ☐ CARING
- ☐ DEPENDABLE
- ☐ COOPERATIVE
- ☐ FRIENDLY
- ☐ ACCURATE
- ☐ CONFIDENT
- ☐ CHEERFUL

- ☐ PATIENT
- ☐ GOOD LISTENER
- ☐ TACTFUL
- ☐ ORGANIZED
- ☐ PERSISTENT
- ☐ FLEXIBLE
- ☐ SENSITIVE
- ☐ MOTIVATED

Add any traits you possess that are not on the list:

_____   _____

_____   _____

_____   _____

_____   _____

Go back over the list and circle the traits you did not check but would like to possess. Work on developing these traits.

GOALS

Give yourself direction. You are responsible for your life.

Organize and prioritize your goals.

Always make realistic and attainable goals.

List obstacles that may get in the way.

Set more goals once you reach your goal.

SESSION 6
SKILLS FOR SUCCESS

Purpose:

To encourage students to set goals for academic improvement

Materials Required:

For the leader:
- ☐ *Group Opening* (page 9)
- ☐ *Group Rules* (page 10)
- ☐ Materials for *Energizer 6* (page 25)
- ☐ Chalkboard and chalk or dry-erase board and marker

For each student:
- ☐ Student's folder
- ☐ *Goals* (from Session 5)
- ☐ *Specific-Subject Goals* (page 210)
- ☐ Pencil

Preparation:

Read the instructions for *Energizer 6*. Gather and prepare the necessary materials.

Make a copy of *Specific-Subject Goals* for each student.

Session Content:

- Give each student his/her folder.

- Select a student to read the *Group Opening*.

- Pass the *Group Rules* around. Have each student read one rule aloud until all of the rules have been read.

- Present *Energizer 6*.

- Review the criteria for setting goals using the *Goals* sheet from Session 5.

- Introduce short- and long-term goals by saying:

    There are short-term and long-term goals. Can you tell me the difference? (Short-term goals are ones you can achieve in the near future—in a day, a week, or a few months. Long-term goals are ones you can achieve over a longer period of time—one semester, one year, five years, or more. Long-term goals are most often our most meaningful and important goals.)

    What would be an example of a short-term goal? (Getting good grade on a test, etc.)

    What are some examples of long-term goals? (Making the basketball team, working toward a future career, etc.)

- Emphasize the importance of goal-setting by saying:

    Setting goals helps you learn new things, acquire new skills, or improve upon existing skills.

    It is important to recognize obstacles that could stand between you and your goal so that you can overcome or avoid those obstacles. Once you list the obstacles to your goal, figure out how to avoid or overcome them.

Set a deadline for reaching your goal. Once you have reached your goal, evaluate it. Make changes and adjustments if necessary.

Once you reach your goal, set more goals.

Take a few minutes to review your goals each day.

- Show the students how to write goals. On the board, make the following chart. Leave the area for *obstacles* and *solutions* blank. Ask the students to tell you what the obstacles are and solutions to each goal. Write their contributions on the board.

- Give each student a copy of *Specific-Subject Goals* and a pencil. Have the students complete the activity sheet, then share their answers with the group.

- Have the students place their activity sheets in their folders. Collect the folders.

GOAL	OBSTACLES	SOLUTIONS
Short-term goal: Get a *B* on next science test	No study hall	Begin studying earlier, instead of the night before the test.
Long-term goal: Go to college	No money	Get a job and save.
		Look for scholarships and grants.
		Have your counselor help you find colleges that employ students to reduce the cost of tuition.

SPECIFIC-SUBJECT GOALS

The academic subject in which I am having the most difficulty is _____.

Write goals so that you can be more successful in that subject.

_____
_____
_____
_____
_____

What are some obstacles that might keep you from reaching your goals?

_____
_____
_____
_____
_____

List ways to overcome or avoid obstacles.

_____
_____
_____
_____
_____

I will accomplish these goals by _____.

_____   _____
SIGNATURE   DATE

SESSION 7
SKILLS FOR SUCCESS

Purpose:
To introduce time-management

Materials Required:

For the leader:
- ☐ *Group Opening* (page 9)
- ☐ *Group Rules* (page 10)
- ☐ Materials for *Energizer 3* (page 22)
- ☐ Chalkboard and chalk or dry-erase board and marker

For each student:
- ☐ Student's folder
- ☐ *Things I Began But Did Not Finish* (page 213)
- ☐ *Priority Worksheet* (page 214)
- ☐ Pencil

Preparation:

Read the instructions for *Energizer 3*. Gather the necessary materials.

Make a copy of *Things I Began But Did Not Finish* and *Priority Worksheet* for each student.

Session Content:

- Give each student his/her folder.

- Select a student to read the *Group Opening*.

- Pass the *Group Rules* around. Have each student read one rule aloud until all of the rules have been read.

- Present *Energizer 3*.

- On the board, write *Time-Management*. Underneath it, write *You are the master of your time. Use it wisely!*

- Ask the students to explain the meaning of the words written on the board. Emphasize that the students have the power to take control of their time and how they manage it is important.

- Give each student a copy of *Things I Began But Did Not Finish* and a pencil. Have the students complete the top part of the activity sheet, then discuss the students' answers.

- Continue the discussion by talking about stumbling blocks. Ask the students to name some possible stumbling blocks to managing time. Write the students' suggestions on the board. Possible answers include:

  – Being disorganized
  – Having a "don't care" attitude
  – Getting distracted
  – Procrastinating
  – Being impatient
  – Over-scheduling

- Then ask the students to suggest what might happen if stumbling blocks are not overcome. Write their suggestions on the board. Possible answers include:

  – Bad grades
  – Low self-esteem
  – Bad attitude
  – Anxiety
  – Stress

- Have the students complete the bottom half of the activity sheet.

- Brainstorm ways to manage time wisely. List the students' ideas on the board. Add the following to the list if they are not mentioned:

    - Keep a daily/weekly planner of things to accomplish
    - Keep a record of what you accomplished
    - Stay focused

- Give the students the following tips for managing time:

    - Do the hardest things first.
    - Prioritize what needs to be done.
    - Break work into smaller tasks.
    - Make a time and place to do your work.

- Give each student a copy of *Priority Worksheet*. Have the students complete the activity sheet, then discuss their lists.

- Tell the students bring their *Priority Worksheet* to the next session. At that time, review what each student has accomplished.

- Remind the students: *Motivation Comes From Yourself!*

- Have the students place their activity sheets in their folders. Collect the folders.

THINGS I BEGAN BUT DID NOT FINISH

Directions: Think about the last few weeks. What things did you begin but not finish? On the on the left side of the book, list the things that you started. On the right side, write why you did not finish what you started.

Notice the stumbling blocks that got in the way of finishing what you began. After our discussion, complete the rest of this activity sheet.

WHAT ARE THE STUMBLING BLOCKS THAT GOT IN YOUR WAY?

_____
_____
_____
_____
_____
_____

PRIORITY WORKSHEET

Directions: List what you must accomplish this week. Then prioritize each task. Write what might prevent you from getting things done. Check off each task when it is completed.

TO-DO LIST

	PRIORITY	COMPLETED
_____	☐	☐
_____	☐	☐
_____	☐	☐
_____	☐	☐
_____	☐	☐
_____	☐	☐
_____	☐	☐
_____	☐	☐
_____	☐	☐
_____	☐	☐
_____	☐	☐
_____	☐	☐
_____	☐	☐
_____	☐	☐
_____	☐	☐

What might prevent you from finishing?

_____
_____
_____
_____

SESSION 8
SKILLS FOR SUCCESS

Purpose:

To help the students understand the relationship between responsibility and time-management

Materials Required:

For the leader:
- ☐ *Group Opening* (page 9)
- ☐ *Group Rules* (page 10)
- ☐ Materials for *Energizer 7* (page 30)
- ☐ Chalkboard and chalk or dry-erase board and marker

For each student:
- ☐ Student's folder
- ☐ *Priority Worksheet* (from Session 7)
- ☐ *Responsibilities* (page 217)
- ☐ Pencil

For each student group:
- ☐ Paper

Preparation:

Read the instructions for *Energizer 7*. Gather and prepare the necessary materials.

Make a copy of *Responsibilities* for each student.

Session Content:

- Give each student his/her folder.

- Select a student to read the *Group Opening*.

- Pass the *Group Rules* around. Have each student read one rule aloud until all of the rules have been read.

- Present *Energizer 7*.

- Review the *Priority Worksheet* from Session 7. Ask the students to share how well they did in prioritizing and completing their *To Do List*. If they did not complete things, ask them what prevented them from doing so.

- Tell the students:

    Sometimes people avoid responsibility and do not manage their time wisely. Today's session will focus on responsibilities.

- Give each student a copy of *Responsibilities* and a pencil. Have the students complete the activity sheet. Discuss the activity sheets, listing on the board the students' suggestions about why people avoid responsibilities. Some answers may be:

    – Laziness
    – Fear of failure
    – Fear of being criticized
    – Apathy

- Tell the students:

    Putting forth a good effort is an important part of being responsible. Attitude also plays a big part in how people take on responsibilities and set goals. Your attitude affects how you feel and act.

- Divide the students into three groups. Give each group a piece of paper. Number the groups 1, 2, and 3. Ask each group to perform one of the following tasks:

    Group 1:
    List things that a person with a positive attitude might say.

    Group 2:
    List things that a person with a depressed/negative attitude might say.

    Group 3:
    List things that a person with an angry attitude might say.

    Tell the groups how much time they have to complete their lists. When the allotted time has elapsed, ask each group to present its list.

- Continue the session by saying:

    A positive attitude will help a person reach his or her goals. Negative and angry attitudes interfere with reaching goals. Remember to use positive self-talk to change negative thinking into positive thinking.

- Have the students place their activity sheets in their folders. Collect the folders.

RESPONSIBILITIES

Directions: List the responsibilities you have in each category.

RESPONSIBILITIES I HAVE:

AT HOME

_____
_____
_____
_____
_____
_____

AT SCHOOL

_____
_____
_____
_____
_____
_____

IN MY COMMUNITY

_____
_____
_____
_____
_____
_____

FOR MYSELF

_____
_____
_____
_____
_____
_____

Some reasons I avoid responsibilities are _____
_____
_____
_____

Some reasons other people avoid responsibilities are _____
_____
_____
_____

SESSION 9
SKILLS FOR SUCCESS

Purpose:

To help the students realize the relationship between success and study skills

Materials Required:

For the leader:
- ☐ *Group Opening* (page 9)
- ☐ *Group Rules* (page 10)
- ☐ *Energizer 9* (page 31)
- ☐ Chalkboard and chalk or dry-erase board and marker

For each student:
- ☐ Student's folder
- ☐ *Responsibility And Study Skills* (page 219)
- ☐ *Setting Goals For Improvement* (page 220)
- ☐ Pencil

Preparation:

Read the instructions for *Energizer 9*.

Make a copy of *Responsibility And Study Skills* and *Setting Goals For Improvement* for each student.

Session Content:

- Give each student his/her folder.

- Select a student to read the *Group Opening*.

- Pass the *Group Rules* around. Have each student read one rule aloud until all of the rules have been read.

- Present *Energizer 9*.

- Tell the students:

    If good study skills are a sign of responsibility and responsibility leads to success, then good study skills lead to success.

- Give each student a copy of *Responsibility And Study Skills* and a pencil. Have the students complete the activity sheet, then total their scores. Discuss the students' responses.

- Give each student a copy of *Setting Goals For Improvement*. Have the students complete the activity sheet, then share with the group the goals they have set for themselves.

- Have the students name materials they need to help them get organized. Write their answers on the board. Some suggestions could be:

    – Backpack
    – Binders
    – Folders
    – Assignment books/agenda planners
    – Calendar

- Review the tips for study skills:

    – Prioritize work to be done.
    – Break down assignments into smaller parts.
    – Do least-favorite things first.
    – Ask for help.
    – Make good use of class time.
    – Get started.

- Have the students place their activity sheets in their folders. Collect the folders.

RESPONSIBILITY AND STUDY SKILLS

Directions: Put a check (✔) in the column that best describes you. Then count the number of checks in each column, total your score, and see how well you did.

	ALWAYS	SOMETIMES	NEVER
I am satisfied with the way I work.	☐	☐	☐
I like school.	☐	☐	☐
I get along with others.	☐	☐	☐
I take notes in class.	☐	☐	☐
I ask for help.	☐	☐	☐
I complete my assignments on time.	☐	☐	☐
I turn in my homework.	☐	☐	☐
I study for tests.	☐	☐	☐
I write down my assignments.	☐	☐	☐
I make a note when my work is completed.	☐	☐	☐
I use tricks to memorize facts.	☐	☐	☐
I make good use of my time.	☐	☐	☐
I prioritize the work I have to do.	☐	☐	☐
I do my least-favorite work first.	☐	☐	☐
I have materials ready for class.	☐	☐	☐

Always   2 points for each answer
Sometimes   1 point for each answer
Never   0 points for each answer

SUBTOTALS ☐ + ☐ + ☐ =

TOTAL SCORE ☐

SCORE:
23-30   You are a responsible student!
12-22   You are getting there!
Below 12   You have some work to do.

SETTING GOALS FOR IMPROVEMENT

Look at the *Responsibility And Study Skills* that you marked "Never." These are areas in which you need to improve.

List the areas in which you need to improve.

1. _____
2. _____
3. _____
4. _____
5. _____
6. _____
7. _____
8. _____

Write goals for each item listed above, then prioritize your goals.

PRIORITY

☐ Goal: _____
    Obstacles: _____
    Solution: _____

☐ Goal: _____
    Obstacles: _____
    Solution: _____

☐ Goal: _____
    Obstacles: _____
    Solution: _____

☐ Goal: _____
    Obstacles: _____
    Solution: _____

☐ Goal: _____
    Obstacles: _____
    Solution: _____

☐ Goal: _____
    Obstacles: _____
    Solution: _____

☐ Goal: _____
    Obstacles: _____
    Solution: _____

☐ Goal: _____
    Obstacles: _____
    Solution: _____

SESSION 10
SKILLS FOR SUCCESS

Purpose:

To review what has been presented in previous lessons

Materials Required:

For the leader:
- ☐ *Group Opening* (page 9)
- ☐ *Group Rules* (page 10)
- ☐ Materials for *Energizer 8* (page 31)
- ☐ *Bingo Numbers* (pages 42-43)
- ☐ Container

For each student:
- ☐ Student's folder
- ☐ *Goals Bingo* (page 223)
- ☐ Markers or pens of two different-color inks

Preparation:

Read the instructions for *Energizer 8*. Gather the necessary materials.

Make a copy of *Goals Bingo* for each student.

Make a copy of the *Bingo Numbers*. Cut the numbers apart and place them in the container.

Session Content:

- Give each student his/her folder.

- Select a student to read the *Group Opening*.

- Pass the *Group Rules* around. Have each student read one rule aloud until all of the rules have been read.

- Present *Energizer 8*.

- Tell the students:

    We are going to play Goals Bingo. *As we play this game, we will review things we have learned in the past few weeks.*

- Give each student a copy of *Goals Bingo* and markers or pens of two different-color inks. Explain how the students should fill in their bingo cards by saying:

    The letters G O A L S are printed at the top of the columns. Below each letter is a number range. Using one color of ink/marker, fill in each circle in each column with one of the numbers within the indicated range. For example, you may choose 3, 5, 8, 12, and 15 to fill in the circles in the column under the letter G.

- Explain how the game is played by saying:

    I will draw one number at a time from this container. As I draw each number, look at your Goals Bingo *card to see if you have written that number on your card. If you have that number on your card, raise your hand. I will call on you to complete the sentence written in that space. You may then place an X in the box using the other color of ink/marker. The first person to get five X's in a row should call out* Goals Bingo! *He or she will win the game.*

- Play the game.

- Discuss the statements on the *Goals Bingo* cards. Ask the students which were easy to complete and which were difficult.

- Have the students go through their folders and give you any papers they want shredded. They may keep their folders and any papers they want.

- To conclude the group, have the students participate in the *Jelly Roll Squeeze* activity. Have the students stand side by side with their arms around each other's waists. Beginning on one end, tell the students to start to roll toward the other end. The first person should roll toward the second person, the second person should roll toward the third person, the third toward the fourth, on so on. When everyone is curled in, say, "Squeeze" on the count of three.

- Thank the students for taking part in the group, especially for sharing with others.

GOAL S+

#1 – #15 (G)
- One reason why someone fails is …
- I should evaluate my goals because …
- Two strengths I have are …
- A good work habit I have is …
- One benefit of reaching a goal is …

#16 – #30 (O)
- One important thing about setting goals is …
- I could change a negative statement into a positive statement by saying …
- An example of a short-term goal is …
- An example of a long-term goal is …
- One reason it is important to manage time is …

#31 – #45 (A)
- One stumbling block to managing time is …
- A stumbling block can cost me …
- FREE SPACE BINGO
- A person with a positive attitude would say …
- One reason someone would avoid responsibility is …

#46 – #60 (L)
- One responsibility I have at school is …
- One responsibility I have at home is …
- One responsibility I have in the community is …
- One responsibility I have to myself is …
- A person with a negative attitude might say …

#61 – #75 (S+)
- Two things that a responsible student does are …
- Two helpful study skills tips are …
- One thing that can help me be organized is …
- One component of setting a goal is …
- One good study skill tip is …

GRAB BAG GUIDANCE © 2005 MAR∗CO PRODUCTS, INC. 1-800-448-2197

STRESS MANAGEMENT

SESSION 1
STRESS-MANAGEMENT

Purpose:

To introduce the group members to each other, explain the purpose of the group, and emphasize the importance of good listening skills

Materials Required:

For the leader:
- ☐ *Group Opening* (page 9)
- ☐ *Group Rules* (page 10)
- ☐ Materials for *Energizer 1* (page 13)
- ☐ Materials for *Energizer 2* (page 14)

For each student:
- ☐ 2-pocket manila folder
- ☐ Crayons or markers
- ☐ Pencil

Preparation:

If you have not already done so, reproduce the *Group Rules* and *Group Opening*. Laminate the pages if possible.

Read the instructions for *Energizer 1* and *Energizer 2*. Gather and prepare the necessary materials.

Session Content:

- Introduce the *Group Rules* and the *Group Opening* to the students.

- Present *Energizer 1*.

- Give each student a folder, crayons or markers, and a pencil. Tell the students the folders will be used to hold their handouts.

- Instruct the students to write their name on the folder, along with the day and class period the group meets. Allow time for the students to use the crayons or markers to decorate their folders.

- Present *Energizer 2* to reinforce the concept that listening to each other while participating in group sessions is very important.

- Tell the students that many things in the world can cause them stress. When people are under stress, they may be unable to do the things they are capable of doing. This group is about how to handle stress-producing situations.

- Collect the folders. (*Note:* The folders will be collected by the leader at the end of each session. At the final session, the students may keep whatever they want from their folders. Shred anything the students do not want to keep.)

SESSION 2
STRESS-MANAGEMENT

Purpose:

To determine the difference between *good stress* and *bad stress*

Materials Required:

For the leader:
- ☐ *Group Opening* (page 9)
- ☐ *Group Rules* (page 10)
- ☐ Materials for *Energizer 4* (page 23)

For each student:
- ☐ Student's folder
- ☐ *Good Stress/Bad Stress* (page 228)
- ☐ Pencil

For each student group:
- ☐ Paper

Preparation:

Read the instructions for *Energizer 4*. Gather and prepare the necessary materials.

Make a copy of *Good Stress/Bad Stress* for each student.

Session Content:

- Give each student his/her folder.

- Select a student to read the *Group Opening*.

- Pass the *Group Rules* around. Have each student read one rule aloud until all of the rules have been read.

- Present *Energizer 4*.

- Divide the students into three groups. Give each group a piece of paper. Give a pencil to each group member. Number the groups 1, 2, and 3. Ask each group to perform one of the following tasks:

   Group 1:
   Write or draw what stress would look like if it could be seen.

   Group 2:
   Write or draw what stress would smell like if were a thing.

   Group 3:
   Write or draw what stress would sound like if it could be heard.

   Have each group share its answers/drawings.

- Tell the students that stress isn't always a bad thing. Then give each student a copy of *Good Stress/Bad Stress*. Have the students write examples of when stress can be good *(learning music for a recital, practicing for a competition in sports, studying for a test, etc.)* and when it can be bad *(when it interferes with your health or how you function or causes you to not think clearly, etc.)*. Have the students share and discuss their complete activity sheets with the group.

- Have the students place their activity sheets in their folders. Collect the folders.

SESSION 3
STRESS-MANAGEMENT

Purpose:

To allow the students to evaluate their stress levels in familiar situations

Materials Required:

For the leader:
- ☐ *Group Opening* (page 9)
- ☐ *Group Rules* (page 10)
- ☐ Materials for *Energizer 5* (page 24)

For each student:
- ☐ Student's folder
- ☐ *Stress Checklist* (page 230)
- ☐ Pencil

Preparation:

Read the instructions for *Energizer 5*. Gather and prepare the necessary materials.

Make a copy of *Stress Checklist* for each student.

Session Content:

- Give each student his/her folder.

- Select a student to read the *Group Opening*.

- Pass the *Group Rules* around. Have each student read one rule aloud until all of the rules have been read.

- Present *Energizer 5*.

- Give each student a copy of *Stress Checklist* and a pencil. Have the students complete the activity, then discuss their conclusions.

    Optional: Determine which stressful situations students have in common.

- Have the students place their activity sheets in their folders. Collect the folders.

STRESS CHECKLIST

Directions: Rate the sources of your stress. Number 1 means you have low stress, 5 is high stress, and 3 would be average. Put an **X** on the line to show the amount of stress you experience in each situation.

☐	SCHOOL	1 · · · 2 · · · 3 · · · 4 · · · 5
☐	PEER PRESSURE	1 · · · 2 · · · 3 · · · 4 · · · 5
☐	HOME	1 · · · 2 · · · 3 · · · 4 · · · 5
☐	BULLIES	1 · · · 2 · · · 3 · · · 4 · · · 5
☐	TEACHERS	1 · · · 2 · · · 3 · · · 4 · · · 5
☐	WORLD SITUATIONS	1 · · · 2 · · · 3 · · · 4 · · · 5
☐	SPORTS	1 · · · 2 · · · 3 · · · 4 · · · 5
☐	TESTS	1 · · · 2 · · · 3 · · · 4 · · · 5
☐	PUBLIC SPEAKING	1 · · · 2 · · · 3 · · · 4 · · · 5
☐	LOSS	1 · · · 2 · · · 3 · · · 4 · · · 5
☐	DISABILITY	1 · · · 2 · · · 3 · · · 4 · · · 5
☐	FRIENDS	1 · · · 2 · · · 3 · · · 4 · · · 5

Add any other sources of stress not listed above.

☐	_____	1 · · · 2 · · · 3 · · · 4 · · · 5
☐	_____	1 · · · 2 · · · 3 · · · 4 · · · 5
☐	_____	1 · · · 2 · · · 3 · · · 4 · · · 5
☐	_____	1 · · · 2 · · · 3 · · · 4 · · · 5

Rank each situation from most stressful to the least stressful.
Write 1 in the square to indicate the situation you find most stressful, 2 for the next-most stressful, etc.

SESSION 4
STRESS-MANAGEMENT

Purpose:

To help the students determine how stress affects the body

Materials Required:

For the leader:
- ☐ *Group Opening* (page 9)
- ☐ *Group Rules* (page 10)
- ☐ Materials for *Energizer 6* (page 25)

For each student:
- ☐ Student's folder
- ☐ *Body Stress* (page 232)
- ☐ Pencil

Preparation:

Read the instructions for *Energizer 6*. Gather and prepare the necessary materials.

Make a copy of *Body Stress* for each student.

Session Content:

- Give each student his/her folder.

- Select a student to read the *Group Opening*.

- Pass the *Group Rules* around. Have each student read one rule aloud until all of the rules have been read.

- Present *Energizer 6*.

- Give each student a copy of *Body Stress* and a pencil. Have the students complete the activity. Then discuss:

    – How different body parts experience stress

    – Stress-producing situations

    – Consequences of stress

    – The various relaxation techniques used to eliminate stress.

- Have the students place their activity sheets in their folders. Collect the folders.

BODY STRESS

Mark the places on the body where you feel stress.

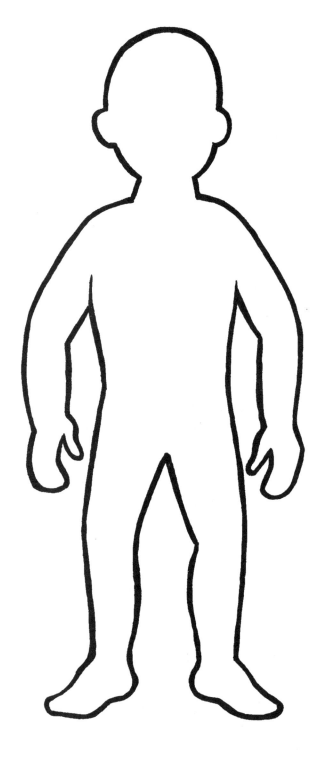

Answer the following:

Physically, I feel stress:

_____
_____
_____
_____

Things that cause me stress:

_____
_____
_____
_____

A lot of stress makes me:

_____
_____
_____
_____

What I do to relax:

_____
_____
_____
_____
_____
_____

SESSION 5
STRESS-MANAGEMENT

Purpose:

To help the students learn ways to cope with stress

Materials Required:

For the leader:
- ☐ *Group Opening* (page 9)
- ☐ *Group Rules* (page 10)
- ☐ *Energizer 15* (page 34)
- ☐ Chalkboard and chalk or dry-erase board and marker

For each student:
- ☐ Student's folder
- ☐ *Stress Busters* (page 234)

Preparation:

Read the instructions for *Energizer 15*.

Make a copy of *Stress Busters* for each student.

Session Content:

- Give each student his/her folder.

- Select a student to read the *Group Opening*.

- Pass the *Group Rules* around. Have each student read one rule aloud until all of the rules have been read.

- Present *Energizer 15*.

- Have the students brainstorm ways to relieve stress. Write their ideas on the board. Discuss the students' suggestions.

- Give each student a copy of *Stress Busters*. Review each suggestion. Suggested discussion format:

    Breathing: Have the students practice the suggestions on the activity sheet.

    Self-Talk: Have several students give examples of self-talk.

    Imagery: Have the students close their eyes for one minute and imagine a relaxing place.

    Exercise: This is self-explanatory.

    Stretching: Have the students try some of the suggested stretches.

    Music: Ask for some examples of relaxing music.

    Know Your Limits: Have the students give examples of "biting off more than you can chew."

    Time-Management: Make a "To-Do" list and check things off as you do them

    Make Time For Fun: Have the students describe things they do for fun.

    Share Your Stress: Have the students name someone with whom they could share their stress.

    Cry: This is self-explanatory

- Review the *Quick Fixes*. Have the students contribute additional *Quick Fixes*.

- Have the students place their activity sheets in their folders. Collect the folders.

STRESS BUSTERS

Breathing—Practice deep, slow breathing. Breathe in through your nose and out through your mouth. Put your hand on your belly and breathe, letting your abdomen rise and fall. Practice deep, slow breathing. This is an excellent anti-stress remedy.

Self-Talk—Talking yourself through a situation is helpful. Remind yourself that you have no control over most things that happen. You can control how you perceive a situation and how you think about it. Tell yourself positive and encouraging things.

Imagery—Imagine things that will be relaxing for you. Some examples are: beach scene with sun, sand, and ocean waves; being on a mountaintop, breathing the fresh air and looking at the beautiful sights around you; bright lights changing to soft colors; blankets piled on you to make you warm and comfortable; a gentle massage, etc.

Exercise—Walking, running, jogging, participating in a sport and working out are all good ways to reduce stress. Along with exercise, eating right is also important.

Stretching—Neck rolls, shoulder rolls, body stretches, and rag doll are all ways to relax tense muscles.

Music—Listen to relaxing music or play a musical instrument for relaxation.

Know Your Limits—Don't "bite off more than you can chew." Be realistic about what you can do and how much time you have.

Time-Management—Make a "To-Do" list and check things off as you do them.

Make Time For Fun—Make sure you take time to have fun. There is a quote that says, "Laugh whenever you can." Laughter is very healthy.

Share Your Stress—Find someone whom you trust and can talk with about what is stressing you.

Cry—It is okay to cry. This can be a healthy way to release your tension.

SOME QUICK FIXES

- Pop bubblewrap.
- Squeeze a tennis ball or stress ball.
- Write down what is bothering you. Then shred the paper.
- Deep breathing.
- Chew bubble gum and blow bubbles.
- Stretch your body, particularly your neck and shoulders.
- Blow bubbles.

Other quick fixes are:

_____

_____

_____

_____

_____

REMEMBER:
You must accept that there are some things you cannot change.
But you *can* change how you think about things.

SESSION 6
STRESS-MANAGEMENT

Purpose:

To help the students learn a new relaxation technique

Materials Required:

For the leader:
- ☐ *Group Opening* (page 9)
- ☐ *Group Rules* (page 10)
- ☐ Materials for *Energizer 18* (page 36)
- ☐ Chalkboard and chalk or dry-erase board and marker

For each student:
- ☐ Student's folder

For each student group:
- ☐ Paper
- ☐ Pencil

Preparation:

Read the instructions for *Energizer 18*. Gather the necessary materials.

Session Content:

- Give each student his/her folder.

- Select a student to read the *Group Opening*.

- Pass the *Group Rules* around. Have each student read one rule aloud until all of the rules have been read.

- Present *Energizer 18*.

- Tell the students that they are going to do a relaxation exercise. Begin the exercise by saying:

    Close your eyes.
    Sit comfortably in your chair.
    Get centered.
    Place your feet on the floor.
    Tighten your feet. Relax them.
    Tighten your calves. Relax them.
    Tighten your thighs. Relax them.
    Tighten your hips. Relax them.
    Tighten your stomach. Relax it.
    Tighten your hands. Relax them.
    Tighten your arms. Relax them.
    Tighten your shoulders. Relax them.
    Tighten your jaw. Relax it.
    Tighten your forehead. Relax it.
    Tighten your entire body. Relax it.
    Open your eyes.

    Have the students describe how they felt about the relaxation activity.

- Divide the students into pairs. Give each pair of students a piece of paper and a pencil. Tell the students to work together to make an acrostic for the word STRESS. Say:

    Write the letters in STRESS vertically on your paper. Think of a letter that begins with each of the letters in the word stress and describes one way a person can handle stress.

    Write the following example on the board.

    S tretch
    T alk
    R elax
    E xercise
    S ilence
    S elf-talk

    Have the students share their acrostics with the group.

- Have the students decide which member of each pair will put the acrostic in his/her folder. Collect the folders.

SESSION 7
STRESS-MANAGEMENT

Purpose:

To have the students make their own stress ball

Materials Required:

For the leader:
- ☐ *Group Opening* (page 9)
- ☐ *Group Rules* (page 10)
- ☐ *Energizer 9* (page 31)
- ☐ Bag of rice or sand
- ☐ Sandwich bag
- ☐ Three 12-15" balloons of various colors
- ☐ Scissors

For each student:
- ☐ Sandwich bag
- ☐ Three 12-15" balloons of various colors
- ☐ Scissors

Preparation:

Read the instructions for *Energizer 9*.

Following the directions found in the session, make a sample stress ball.

Session Content:

- Select a student to read the *Group Opening*.

- Pass the *Group Rules* around. Have each student read one rule aloud until all of the rules have been read.

- Present *Energizer 9*.

- Show the students the sample stress ball. Then say:

    This is a stress ball. Today you are going to make your own stress ball to squeeze when you feel stressed. Squeezing the ball can help lower your stress level.

- Give each student three balloons, scissors, and a sandwich bag. Then give the following instructions:

    1. *Cut off the stem of each balloon. This will leave the round part.*

    2. *(Optional) Cut designs into your balloon.*

    3. *(Pass the bag of rice/sand around.) Fill the bottom of your bag with rice (sand). Lay the bag flat. Then fold the bag down until all you see is the rice (sand). Fold the bag in half.*

    4. *Put one balloon over the bag. Do the same with the second balloon, but going in a different direction. When you add the third balloon, make sure your entire bag is covered.*

    The students have created their own stress ball.

- Conclude the session by having each student describe a personally stressful incident while squeezing his/her stress ball. Tell the students they may take their stress balls with them.

SESSION 8
STRESS-MANAGEMENT

Purpose:

To review what has been presented in previous lessons

Materials Required:

For the leader:
- ☐ *Group Opening* (page 9)
- ☐ *Group Rules* (page 10)
- ☐ Materials for *Energizer 7* (page 30)
- ☐ *Bingo Numbers* (pages 42-43)
- ☐ Container

For each student:
- ☐ Student's folder
- ☐ *Stress Bingo* (page 239)
- ☐ Markers or pens of two different-color inks

Preparation:

Read the instructions for *Energizer 7*. Gather and prepare the necessary materials.

Make a copy of *Stress Bingo* for each student.

Make a copy of the *Bingo Numbers*. Cut the numbers apart and place them in the container.

Session Content:

- Give each student his/her folder.

- Select a student to read the *Group Opening*.

- Pass the *Group Rules* around. Have each student read one rule aloud until all of the rules have been read.

- Present *Energizer 7*.

- Tell the students:

    We are going to play Stress Bingo. *As we play this game, we will review things we have learned in the past few weeks.*

- Give each student a copy of *Stress Bingo* and markers or pens of two different-color inks. Explain how the students should fill in their bingo cards by saying:

    The letters S T R E SS *are printed at the top of the columns. Below each letter is a number range. Using one color of ink/marker, fill in each circle in each column with one of the numbers within the indicated range. For example, you may choose 3, 5, 8, 12, and 15 to fill in the circles in the column under the letter* S.

- Explain how the game is played by saying:

    I will draw one number at a time from this container. As I draw each number, look at your Stress Bingo *card to see if you have written that number on your card. If you have that number on your card, raise your hand. I will call on you to complete the sentence written in that space. You may then place an X in the box using the other color of ink/marker. The first person to get five X's in a row should call out* Stress Bingo! *He or she will win the game.*

- Play the game.

- Discuss the statements on the *Stress Bingo* cards. Ask the students which were easy to complete and which were difficult.

- Have the students place their *Stress Bingo* cards in their folders. Collect the folders.

STRESS FREE

	#1 – #15	#16 – #30	#31 – #45	#46 – #60	#61 – #75
	One thing stress does to me is …	Two things I can do when I feel stressed are …	If stress could be seen, it would look like …	A time when stress can be positive is …	The way Mom/Dad handles stress is …
	One thing that causes me stress is …	In my body, I feel stress …	If stress were a thing, it would smell like …	A time when stress can be negative is …	A stressful event that happened in my life was …
	When I am stressed, I feel …	Two quick fixes for stress are …	FREE SPACE BINGO	A relaxation technique I can use when stressed is …	When creating a quiet scene in my head, I like to go …
	To calm myself down when I am stressed, I …	Something I can do to help avoid stress is …	If stress were a thing, it would act like …	Two stressors in my life are …	Something I can do every day to reduce stress is …
	Someone I could talk with when I am stressed is …	Something that worries me is …	If stress could be heard, it would sound like…	Two ways a person can relax are …	Someone who seems stressed a lot is …

GRAB BAG GUIDANCE © 2005 MAR*CO PRODUCTS, INC. 1-800-448-2197

SESSION 9
STRESS-MANAGEMENT

Purpose:

To bring closure to the group

Materials Required:

For the leader:
- ☐ *Group Opening* (page 9)
- ☐ *Group Rules* (page 10)
- ☐ Materials for *Energizer 10* (page 32)

For each student:
- ☐ Student's folder
- ☐ Index cards
- ☐ Pencil

Preparation:

Read the instructions for *Energizer 10*. Gather the necessary materials.

Session Content:

- Give each student his/her folder and a pencil.

- Select a student to read the *Group Opening*.

- Pass the *Group Rules* around. Have each student read one rule aloud until all of the rules have been read.

- Present *Energizer 10*.

- Give each group member as many index cards as there are students in the group, less one. Feature one group member at a time by having the other students write something nice to him/her. Tell the students to begin with "Dear ____." Make sure each student signs his/her name.

- After each student has been featured, everyone should have an index card from each student in the group. Tell the students they may keep the cards and read them if they ever start feeling low. They may want to display the cards in their bedroom and read them often.

- Have the students go through their folders and give you any papers they want shredded. They may keep their folders and any papers they want.

- To conclude the group, have the students participate in the *Jelly Roll Squeeze* activity. Have the students stand side by side with their arms around each other's waists. Beginning on one end, tell the students to start to roll toward the other end. The first person should roll toward the second person, the second person should roll toward the third person, the third toward the fourth, on so on. When everyone is curled in, say, "Squeeze" on the count of three.

- Thank the students for taking part in the group.

Grab Bag Guidance

GRAB BAG GUIDANCE SESSIONS

Session 1	Group Expectations
Session 2	Getting To Know You
Session 3	Anger-Management
Session 4	Anger-Management Bingo
Session 5	Grief And Loss
Session 6	More On Grief And Loss
Session 7	Grief And Loss Bingo
Session 8	Bullying
Session 9	More On Bullying
Session 10	Stress-Management
Session 11	Stress-Management Bingo
Session 12	Make Your Own Stress Ball
Session 13	Self-Esteem
Session 14	More On Self-Esteem And Self-Worth Bingo
Session 15	Final Group Session

SESSION 1
GROUP EXPECTATIONS

Purpose:

To introduce the group members to each other, explain the purpose of the group, and emphasize the importance of good listening skills

Materials Required:

For the leader:
- ☐ *Group Opening* (page 9)
- ☐ *Group Rules* (page 10)
- ☐ Materials for *Energizer 1* (page 13)
- ☐ Materials for *Energizer 2* (page 14)

For each student:
- ☐ 2-pocket manila folder
- ☐ Crayons or markers
- ☐ Pencil

Preparation:

If you have not already done so, reproduce the *Group Rules* and *Group Opening*. Laminate the pages if possible.

Read the instructions for *Energizer 1* and *Energizer 2*. Gather and prepare the necessary materials.

Session Content:

- Introduce the *Group Rules* and the *Group Opening* to the students.

- Explain that the purpose of the group is to learn about several different topics—anger-management, grief and loss, bullying, stress, and self-esteem.

- Present *Energizer 1*.

- Give each student a folder, crayons or markers, and a pencil. Tell the students the folders will be used to hold their handouts.

- Instruct the students to write their name on the folder, along with the day and class period the group meets. Allow time for the students to use the crayons or markers to decorate their folders.

- Present *Energizer 2* to reinforce the concept that listening to each other while participating in group sessions is very important.

- Collect the folders. (*Note:* The folders will be collected by the leader at the end of each session. At the final session, the students may keep whatever they want from their folders. Shred anything the students do not want to keep.)

SESSION 2
GETTING TO KNOW YOU

Purpose:

To help the students become better acquainted with other group members

Materials Required:

For the leader:
- ☐ *Group Opening* (page 9)
- ☐ *Group Rules* (page 10)
- ☐ Materials for *Energizer 4* (page 23)

For each student:
- ☐ Student's folder
- ☐ *Getting To Know You* (page 245)
- ☐ Pencil

Preparation:

Read the instructions for *Energizer 4*. Gather and prepare the necessary materials.

Make a copy of *Getting To Know You* for each student.

Session Content:

- Give each student his/her folder.

- Select a student to read the *Group Opening*.

- Pass the *Group Rules* around. Have each student read one rule aloud until all of the rules have been read.

- Present *Energizer 4*.

- Give each student a copy of *Getting To Know You* and a pencil. Tell the students to complete the unfinished sentences on the activity sheet.

- Have the students share whatever they have written on their activity sheets and are comfortable sharing. Encourage the students to provide feedback to one another.

- Have the students place their activity sheets in their folders. Collect the folders.

GETTING TO KNOW YOU

Directions: Complete each of the unfinished sentences.

If I had three wishes, I would wish for _____

_____

_____

_____ .

My favorite thing to do is _____ .

Something that I don't like is _____ .

If I had $500.00, I would _____

_____ .

A good time I had with my family was _____

_____ .

A bad time I had with my family was _____

_____ .

Something I am good at is _____

_____ .

If I could visit any place it would be _____ .

Someone I would like to meet is _____ .

One thing I like about my best friend is _____ .

When I grow up, I would like to be _____ .

Something you probably don't know about me is _____

_____ .

GRAB BAG GUIDANCE © 2005 MAR*CO PRODUCTS, INC. 1-800-448-2197

245

SESSION 3
ANGER-MANAGEMENT

Purpose:

To help the students learn healthy ways to express anger

Materials Required:

For the leader:
- ☐ *Group Opening* (page 9)
- ☐ *Group Rules* (page 10)
- ☐ Materials for *Energizer 7* (page 30)
- ☐ Chart paper and marker
- ☐ Chalkboard and chalk or dry-erase board and marker

For each student:
- ☐ Student's folder
- ☐ *Anger* (page 248)
- ☐ Pencil

Preparation:

Read the instructions for *Energizer 7*. Gather and prepare the necessary materials.

Make a copy of *Anger* for each student

Session Content:

- Give each student his/her folder.

- Select a student to read the *Group Opening*.

- Pass the *Group Rules* around. Have each student read one rule aloud until all of the rules have been read.

- Present *Energizer 7*.

- Write the letters *ANGER* on the board. Then say:

    Anger is only one letter away from danger.

    Add the letter *D* to the front of *ANGER* to spell *DANGER*. Then say:

    Everyone gets angry. What is important is how you handle your anger.

- Give each student a copy of *Anger* and a pencil. Emphasize that people don't always handle anger the same way. Have the students complete the activity sheet.

- On the chart paper, write several ways people handle anger. Examples may be *cry, yell,* and *talk with someone*. Then ask the students to share with the group ways that they handle anger. List all the ways mentioned on the chart paper. Then add any of the ideas listed below. Tell the students that these are ways other students have told you they handle anger. Be sure to add healthy ways to the list. Allow the students to add ways they have seen others handle anger.

    Below are some examples of what students often say:

cry	talk with someone
yell	go to your bedroom
hit	kick
read	write
throw things	punch something
draw	leave
call a friend	take a walk

eat
exercise
play sports
watch TV
count to 10
jog
spread rumors
drive fast
break things
play videogames

- Once the list is complete, tell the students:

    These are three rules for handling anger.

    1. *Don't hurt yourself.*
    2. *Don't hurt someone else.*
    3. *Don't damage or destroy property.*

- Have the students cross out the suggestions on the list that would hurt them or someone else and the suggestions that would damage or destroy property. Circle the other suggestions.

- Tell the students:

    Look at the suggestions that are circled. These are healthy ways of handling anger. When we are angry, each of us can choose to react in a healthy or unhealthy manner.

- Title the chart *Healthy And Unhealthy Reactions To Anger*. Tell the students they now know how to handle their anger in a healthy manner.

- Have the students put their activity sheets in their folders. Collect the folders.

ANGER

Three ways I act when I am angry are:

_____

_____

_____

I get angry when my mom _____

_____.

I get angry when my dad _____

_____.

I get angry when my best friend _____

_____.

I get angry when my teacher _____

_____.

If other people saw me when I am angry, they would __

_____.

Five things, other than people, that make me angry are:

1. _____
2. _____
3. _____
4. _____
5. _____

SESSION 4
ANGER-MANAGEMENT BINGO

Purpose:

To review the rules of anger-management and healthy strategies for coping with anger

Materials Required:

For the leader:
- ☐ *Group Opening* (page 9)
- ☐ *Group Rules* (page 10)
- ☐ *Energizer 9* (page 31)
- ☐ *Bingo Numbers* (pages 42-43)
- ☐ Container

For each student:
- ☐ Student's folder
- ☐ *Anger Bingo* (page 251)
- ☐ Markers or pens of two different-color inks

Preparation:

Read the instructions for *Energizer 9*.

Make a copy of *Anger Bingo* for each student.

Make a copy of the *Bingo Numbers*. Cut the numbers apart and place them in the container.

Session Content:

- Give each student his/her folder.

- Select a student to read the *Group Opening*.

- Pass the *Group Rules* around. Have each student read one rule aloud until all of the rules have been read.

- Present *Energizer 9*.

- Review the rules for anger and the healthy strategies for coping with anger.

- Have the students take turns discussing any situations that happened during the past week in which the student relied on his/her knowledge of handling anger in a healthy way.

- Tell the students:

   We are going to play Anger Bingo. *As we play this game, we will review things we have learned.*

- Give each student a copy of *Anger Bingo* and markers or pens of two different-color inks. Explain how the students should fill in their bingo cards by saying:

   The letters A N G E R *are printed at the top of the columns. Below each letter is a number range. Using one color of ink/marker, fill in each circle in each column with one of the numbers within the indicated range. For example, you may choose 3, 5, 8, 12, and 15 to fill in the circles in the column under the letter* A.

- Explain how the game is played by saying:

  I will draw one number at a time from this container. As I draw each number, look at your Anger Bingo *card to see if you have written that number on your card. If you have that number on your card, raise your hand. I will call on you to complete the sentence written in that space. You may then place an X in the box using the other color of ink/marker. The first person to get five X's in a row should call out* Anger Bingo! *He or she will win the game.*

- Play the game.

- Discuss the statements on the *Anger Bingo* cards. Ask the students which were easy to complete and which were difficult.

- Have the students put their activity sheets in their folders. Collect the folders.

ANGER BINGO

A #1 – #15	N #16 – #30	G #31 – #45	E #46 – #60	R #61 – #75
When I am angry, I feel …	One place in my body I feel anger is …	My anger is like …	One thing that makes me angry is …	One healthy way to handle anger is …
I know when someone is angry because …	When a person is angry, his/her face looks …	I know when someone is angry and says nothing because …	Something someone says or does that makes me angry is …	I get angry when other kids …
One unhealthy way to handle anger is …	One thing I can do to control my anger is …	FREE SPACE BINGO	I get angry when adults …	One unhealthy way to handle anger is …
The last time I was angry was …	One way I act when I am angry is …	When I am angry, I …	If other people saw me when I am angry, they would …	When I am angry, my mom/dad …
One person I can talk with when I am angry is …	Three rules for handling anger are …	Before I react to an anger-provoking situation, I …	One healthy way to handle anger is …	Anger is one letter away from …

GRAB BAG GUIDANCE © 2005 MAR*CO PRODUCTS, INC. 1-800-448-2197

SESSION 5
GRIEF AND LOSS

Purpose:

To help students understand the meaning of *loss* and recognize feelings associated with loss

Materials Required:

For the leader:
- ☐ *Group Opening* (page 9)
- ☐ *Group Rules* (page 10)
- ☐ Materials for *Energizer 6* (page 25)
- ☐ Chart paper and marker

For each student:
- ☐ Student's folder
- ☐ Paper
- ☐ Pencil

Preparation:

Read the instructions for *Energizer 6*. Gather and prepare the necessary materials.

Title a piece of chart paper *Feelings Word Chart*.

Session Content:

- Give each student his/her folder.

- Select a student to read the *Group Opening*.

- Pass the *Group Rules* around. Have each student read one rule aloud until all of the rules have been read.

- Present *Energizer 6*.

- Explain the following to the students:

    Whenever you feel like someone or something is missing from your life, you experience loss. This occurs not only when someone dies, but also when a friend moves away or you move away from friends. You can feel loss when a pet dies or parents divorce.

- Give each student paper and a pencil. Tell the students to make a list of people or pets they had in their life and have lost. Have the students share their lists with the group.

- Tell the students:

    There are no good or bad feelings. People may feel differently about a situation, and that is okay. The important thing is to feel something.

- Ask the students to name all the feeling words associated with loss that they can think of. Write the words on the chart paper. Discuss each word the students suggest. Examples include:

    | confused | hurt | sad |
    | nervous | depressed | sick |
    | angry | terrible | betrayed |
    | frustrated | lonely | alone |
    | ignored | scared | annoyed |
    | anxious | withdrawn | worried |

    Save the chart for the next session.

- Have the students put their lists in their folders. Collect the folders.

SESSION 6
MORE ON GRIEF AND LOSS

Purpose:

To have students examine feelings experienced at the time of the loss and to understand the healing process

Materials Required:

For the leader:
- ☐ *Group Opening* (page 9)
- ☐ *Group Rules* (page 10)
- ☐ Materials for *Energizer 14* (page 34)
- ☐ *Feelings Word Chart* (from previous session)
- ☐ Chalkboard and chalk or dry-erase board and marker
- ☐ Masking tape

For each student:
- ☐ Student's folder
- ☐ *Colors Of My Heart* (page 255)
- ☐ Pencil
- ☐ Crayons or markers

Preparation:

Read the instructions for *Energizer 14*. Gather the necessary materials.

Make a copy of *Colors Of My Heart* for each student.

Session Content:

- Give each student his/her folder.

- Select a student to read the *Group Opening*.

- Pass the *Group Rules* around. Have each student read one rule aloud until all of the rules have been read.

- Present *Energizer 14*.

- Hang the *Feelings Word Chart* from the previous session on the wall. Give each student a copy of *Colors Of My Heart*, a pencil, and crayons or markers. Then say:

   Think back to how you felt at the time of your loss. Using crayons (markers), color the heart. Use four or five colors that represent your feelings. At the bottom of your paper, write the name of the color and the feeling word it represents. You may refer to the Feelings Word Chart *we made in the last session.*

   Have the students share their work with the group.

- Then say:

   There is no set time in which a person heals after losing a loved one.

   Go to the board and draw a straight line like the one below.

   ☹———————☺

   Then say:

   You don't go in a straight line from feeling sad to feeling happy again.

The healing process is more like a jagged line.

Draw a jagged line like the one below.

Then say:

There will be days when you will feel down and sad. On other days, you will feel fine and happy. You will have your ups and downs and even go backward sometimes. This behavior will last for a period of time. It is normal.

- Explain that some people think that people who experience loss go through three stages:

  1. Shock and/or disbelief
  2. Anger and/or depression
  3. Acceptance and moving on

Explain each stage to the students. Ask the students if they see themselves as going through any of these stages. Discuss their responses. Then say:

Most people seem to experience these stages. How long you stay in stages one or two is different for each person.

- Have the students put their activity sheets in their folders. Collect the folders.

COLORS OF MY HEART

SESSION 7
GRIEF AND LOSS BINGO

Purpose:

To encourage the students to verbalize their thoughts about grief and loss

Materials Required:

For the leader:
- ☐ *Group Opening* (page 9)
- ☐ *Group Rules* (page 10)
- ☐ *Energizer 16* (page 35)
- ☐ *Bingo Numbers* (pages 42-43)
- ☐ Container

For each student:
- ☐ Student's folder
- ☐ *Grief Bingo* (page 257)
- ☐ Markers or pens of two different-color inks

Preparation:

Read the instructions for *Energizer 16*.

Make a copy of *Grief Bingo* for each student.

Make a copy of the *Bingo Numbers*. Cut the numbers apart and place them in the container.

Session Content:

- Give each student his/her folder.

- Select a student to read the *Group Opening*.

- Pass the *Group Rules* around. Have each student read one rule aloud until all of the rules have been read.

- Present *Energizer 16*.

- Tell the students they are going to play *Grief Bingo*. Give each student a copy of *Grief Bingo* and markers or pens of two different-color inks. Explain how the students should fill in their bingo cards by saying:

    The letters G R I E F are printed at the top of the columns. Below each letter is a number range. Using one color of ink/marker, fill in each circle in each column with one of the numbers within the indicated range. For example, you may choose 3, 5, 8, 12, and 15 to fill in the circles in the column under the letter G.

- Explain how the game is played by saying:

    I will draw one number at a time from this container. As I draw each number, look at your Grief Bingo *card to see if you have written that number on your card. If you have that number on your card, raise your hand. I will call on you to complete the sentence written in that space. You may then place an X in the box using the other color of ink/marker. The first person to get five X's in a row should call out* Grief Bingo! *He or she will win the game.*

- Play the game.

- Discuss the statements on the *Grief Bingo* cards.

- Have the students put their bingo cards in their folders. Collect the folders.

GRIEF

	G #1 – #15	**R** #16 – #30	**I** #31 – #45	**E** #46 – #60	**F** #61 – #75
○	Someone I loved and have lost is …	A color that represents my feeling of loss is …	A good time I had with my loved one was …	If only …	If I could spend one more day with my loved one, I would …
○	Some feelings I had when I lost my loved one were …	I can accept …	A funny thing that happened with my loved one was …	I am sorry that …	Three feeling words that describe loss are …
○	The hardest thing about losing someone is …	I cannot accept …	FREE SPACE **BINGO**	Sometimes I am afraid …	Three stages of grief are …
○	I'd like to tell the person I lost …	If I could have done things differently …	I wish …	I often worry about …	My favorite memory of my loved one is …
○	I don't understand …	Three words that describe my loved one are …	I like to talk about my loved one with …	Something that has changed in my family since my loss is …	The future …

GRAB BAG GUIDANCE © 2005 MAR∗CO PRODUCTS, INC. 1-800-448-2197

SESSION 8
BULLYING

Purpose:

To encourage the students to verbalize their thoughts about bullying

Materials Required:

For the leader:
- ☐ *Group Opening* (page 9)
- ☐ *Group Rules* (page 10)
- ☐ Materials for *Energizer 3* (page 22)
- ☐ Chart paper and marker
- ☐ Masking tape

Preparation:

Read the instructions for *Energizer 3*. Gather the necessary materials.

Title four sheets of chart paper:

1. What is bullying?
2. What do bullies do?
3. What are the reasons kids get picked on?
4. Where does bullying take place?

Attach the four titled charts and one blank piece of chart paper to the wall with tape.

Session Content:

- Select a student to read the *Group Opening*.

- Pass the *Group Rules* around. Have each student read one rule aloud until all of the rules have been read.

- Present *Energizer 3*.

- Tell the students:

    There are five pieces of chart paper hanging on the wall. Four have titles. We are going to discuss each title, then make a list of what you believe would explain each title. The extra piece of chart paper is for our notes about the first question: What is bullying?

- Begin with the *What is bullying?* chart. Have the students tell the group what they believe bullying is. Record their answers on the blank piece of chart paper. Then have the students compile their ideas into one definition of *bullying*. Write that definition on the chart paper. It should be something like:

    Bullying is intentionally aggressive behavior. It is made up of repeated harmful acts that include an imbalance of power. Bullying is the most common form of violence. It is hurtful to the victim.

- Continue with the other three charts, asking the students to contribute answers to each question. Have the students record these answers directly on the chart paper. Discuss the students' answers.

- Conclude the session by saying:

    Not all teasing *is* bullying. *How the person perceives the teasing, if the negative act is repeated, and if the bully has power over the victim are all deciding factors. It is important to stop verbal bullying when it occurs so it does not become physical. You shouldn't say negative things about another person.*

SESSION 9
MORE ON BULLYING

Purpose:

To provide strategies for students to use when they are bullying victims or witnesses

Materials Required:

For the leader:
- ☐ *Group Opening* (page 9)
- ☐ *Group Rules* (page 10)

Preparation:

None

Session Content:

- Select a student to read the *Group Opening*.

- Pass the *Group Rules* around. Have each student read one rule aloud until all of the rules have been read.

- Tell the students:

    Bullies are sneaky. They can humiliate you. They can hurt you. And sometimes you are the one who gets in trouble, not the bully. Today, we are going to learn some things you can say or do to take power away from a bully.

- Have the students practice the first bully-diffusing technique by saying:

    I would like you to stand up and put your shoulders back. Take a deep breath. Keep your head up. Cross your arms in front of you. Look confident. Say nothing. This is one technique you can use when you are dealing with a bully. When it is just the bully and you, the bully may go away if you do this. If the bully has support and you have no one to support you, use another strategy.

- Tell the students to sit down. Continue the session by presenting the second bully-diffusing technique. Say:

    Another strategy is to agree with the bully. Let's practice this. I need two volunteers.

    Select two volunteers. Have one volunteer role-play the bully. Have the other volunteer pretend to be the victim. Say:

    As a bully, you are to say, "You look like a nerd." As the victim, answer, "Yeah, I do look like a nerd," then walk away.

    Have the volunteers perform the role-play. Then ask the students to suggest other scenarios. Using the students suggestions, have them take turns role-playing this technique.

- Present the third bully-diffusing technique by saying:

    A third strategy is to simply laugh at the bully and walk away. Let's practice this. I need two volunteers.

Select two volunteers. Have one volunteer role-play the bully. Have the other volunteer pretend to be the victim. Say:

As a bully, you are to say, "You look like a nerd." As the victim, just laugh and walk away.

- Have the volunteers perform the role-play. Then ask the students to suggest other scenarios. Using the students suggestions, have them take turns role-playing this technique.

- Continue the session by saying:

    If you are a member of a group and you see someone being bullied, one person must get help. The rest of the witnesses must stand tall with heads up, arms crossed, staring at the bully, but saying nothing. This takes the power away from the bully and is certainly more effective than a group standing around watching, and worse than this, cheering. When kids do that, they give the bully the power he or she craves.

- Conclude the session by reminding the students:

    When bullies do not get the response they want and are given no power, they will stop.

    Remember: If you are being bullied, or see someone else being bullied, seek help. There are many support persons in the school who can help you. Let your parents and your teacher or counselor know what is happening.

Additional Activity:

- This would require another session, but would be well worth it. Show the students the video *Joey* (available from Mar*co Products). It is an excellent half-hour video and, with additional time allotted for discussion, is a good example of the importance of eliminating bullying.

SESSION 10
STRESS-MANAGEMENT

Purpose:

To help the students learn ways to cope with stress

Materials Required:

For the leader:
- ☐ *Group Opening* (page 9)
- ☐ *Group Rules* (page 10)
- ☐ *Energizer 15* (page 34)
- ☐ Materials for *Energizer 18* (page 36)
- ☐ Chalkboard and chalk or dry-erase board and marker

For each student:
- ☐ Student's folder
- ☐ *Stress Busters* (page 263)
- ☐ Pencil

For each student group:
- ☐ Paper

Preparation:

Read the instructions for *Energizer 15* and *Energizer 18*. Gather the necessary materials.

Make a copy of *Stress Busters* for each student.

Session Content:

- Give each student his/her folder.

- Select a student to read the *Group Opening*.

- Pass the *Group Rules* around. Have each student read one rule aloud until all of the rules have been read.

- Present *Energizer 15*. After completing the energizer, tell the students that this exercise is one way they can try to relieve some of their stress.

- Divide the students into three groups. Give each group a piece of paper. Give a pencil to each group member. Number the groups 1, 2, and 3. Ask each group to perform one of the following tasks:

    Group 1:
    Write or draw what stress would look like if it could be seen.

    Group 2:
    Write or draw what stress would smell like if were a thing.

    Group 3:
    Write or draw what stress would sound like if it could be heard.

    Have each group share its answers/drawings.

- Ask the students following questions:

    What is stress?

    Physically, where do you feel stress? (stomach, jaw, head, etc.)

    What kind of things cause stress? (tests, team tryouts, home problems, etc.)

What are some consequences of a lot of stress? (health problems, poor performance, etc.)

As the students give their responses, write them on the board.

- Point out that in some cases, stress may be good. An example is studying for a test or learning music for a recital. Ask the students for other examples of times when stress can be good.

- Give each student a copy of *Stress Busters*. Review each suggestion in detail making sure the students clearly understand each method. Ask the students for additional suggestions. Suggested discussion format:

    Breathing: Have the students practice the suggestions on the activity sheet.

    Self-Talk: Have several students give examples of self-talk.

    Imagery: Have the students close their eyes for one minute and imagine a relaxing place.

    Exercise: This is self-explanatory.

    Stretching: Have the students try some of the suggested stretches.

    Music: Ask for some examples of relaxing music.

    Know Your Limits: Have the students give examples of "biting off more than you can chew."

    Time-Management: Make a "To-Do" list and check things off as you do them

    Make Time For Fun: Have the students describe things they do for fun.

    Share Your Stress: Have the students name someone with whom they could share their stress.

    Cry: This is self-explanatory

- Review the *Quick Fixes*. Have the students contribute additional *Quick Fixes*. Tell the students to write these ideas on their activity sheet.

- Conclude the session by presenting *Energizer 18*.

- Have the students place their activity sheets in their folders. Collect the folders.

STRESS BUSTERS

Breathing—Practice deep, slow breathing. Breathe in through your nose and out through your mouth. Put your hand on your belly and breathe, letting your abdomen rise and fall. Practice deep, slow breathing. This is an excellent anti-stress remedy.

Self-Talk—Talking yourself through a situation is helpful. Remind yourself that you have no control over most things that happen. You can control how you perceive a situation and how you think about it. Tell yourself positive and encouraging things.

Imagery—Imagine things that will be relaxing for you. Some examples are: beach scene with sun, sand, and ocean waves; being on a mountaintop, breathing the fresh air and looking at the beautiful sights around you; bright lights changing to soft colors; blankets piled on you to make you warm and comfortable; a gentle massage, etc.

Exercise—Walking, running, jogging, participating in a sport and working out are all good ways to reduce stress. Along with exercise, eating right is also important.

Stretching—Neck rolls, shoulder rolls, body stretches, and rag doll are all ways to relax tense muscles.

Music—Listen to relaxing music or play a musical instrument for relaxation.

Know Your Limits—Don't "bite off more than you can chew." Be realistic about what you can do and how much time you have.

Time-Management—Make a "To-Do" list and check things off as you do them.

Make Time For Fun—Make sure you take time to have fun. There is a quote that says, "Laugh whenever you can." Laughter is very healthy.

Share Your Stress—Find someone whom you trust and can talk with about what is stressing you.

Cry—It is okay to cry. This can be a healthy way to release your tension.

SOME QUICK FIXES

- Pop bubblewrap.
- Squeeze a tennis ball or stress ball.
- Write down what is bothering you. Then shred the paper.
- Deep breathing.
- Chew bubble gum and blow bubbles.
- Stretch your body, particularly your neck and shoulders.
- Blow bubbles.

Other quick fixes are:

_____

_____

_____

_____

_____

⭐☆ REMEMBER:

You must accept that there are some things you cannot change. But you *can* change how you think about things.

SESSION 11
STRESS-MANAGEMENT BINGO

Purpose:

To review what has been presented in previous sessions

Materials Required:

For the leader:
- ☐ *Group Opening* (page 9)
- ☐ *Group Rules* (page 10)
- ☐ Materials for *Energizer 5* (page 24)
- ☐ *Bingo Numbers* (pages 42-43)
- ☐ Container

For each student:
- ☐ Student's folder
- ☐ *Stress Bingo* (page 265)
- ☐ Markers or pens of two different-color inks

Preparation:

Read the instructions for *Energizer 5*. Gather and prepare the necessary materials.

Make a copy of *Stress Bingo* for each student.

Make a copy of the *Bingo Numbers*. Cut the numbers apart and place them in the container.

Session Content:

- Give each student his/her folder.

- Select a student to read the *Group Opening*.

- Pass the *Group Rules* around. Have each student read one rule aloud until all of the rules have been read.

- Present *Energizer 5*.

- Tell the students they are going to play *Stress Bingo*. Give each student a copy of *Stress Bingo* and markers or pens of two different-color inks. Explain how the students should fill in their bingo cards by saying:

    The letters S T R E SS are printed at the top of the columns. Below each letter is a number range. Using one color of ink/marker, fill in each circle in each column with one of the numbers within the indicated range. For example, you may choose 3, 5, 8, 12, and 15 to fill in the circles in the column under the letter S.

- Explain how the game is played. Say:

    I will draw one number at a time from this container. As I draw each number, look at your Stress Bingo card to see if you have written that number on your card. If you have that number on your card, raise your hand. I will call on you to complete the sentence written in that space. You may then place an X in the box using the other color of ink/marker. The first person to get five X's in a row should call out Stress Bingo! *He or she will win the game.*

- Play the game.

- Discuss the statements on the *Stress Bingo* cards.

- Have the students put their bingo cards in their folders. Collect the folders.

STRESS

S #1 – #15	T #16 – #30	R #31 – #45	E #46 – #60	S #61 – #75
One thing stress does to me is …	Two things I can do when I feel stressed are …	If stress could be seen, it would look like …	A time when stress can be positive is …	The way Mom/Dad handles stress is …
One thing that causes me stress is …	In my body, I feel stress …	If stress were a thing, it would smell like …	A time when stress can be negative is …	A stressful event that happened in my life is …
When I am stressed, I feel …	Two quick fixes for stress are …	FREE SPACE BINGO	A relaxation technique I can use when stressed is …	When creating a quiet scene in my head, I like to go …
To calm myself down when I am stressed, I …	Something I can do to help avoid stress is …	If stress were a thing, it would act like …	Two stressors in my life are …	Something I can do every day to reduce stress is …
Someone I could talk with when I am stressed is …	Something that worries me is …	If stress could be heard, it would sound like…	Two ways a person can relax are …	Someone who seems stressed a lot is …

SESSION 12
MAKE YOUR OWN STRESS BALL

Purpose:

To have the students make their own stress ball

Materials Required:

For the leader:
- ☐ *Group Opening* (page 9)
- ☐ *Group Rules* (page 10)
- ☐ Bag of rice or sand
- ☐ Sandwich bag
- ☐ Three 12-15" balloons of various colors
- ☐ Scissors

For each student:
- ☐ Sandwich bag
- ☐ Three 12-15" balloons of various colors
- ☐ Scissors

Preparation:

Following the directions found in the session, make a sample stress ball.

Session Content:

- Select a student to read the *Group Opening*.

- Pass the *Group Rules* around. Have each student read one rule aloud until all of the rules have been read.

- Show the students the sample stress ball. Then say:

    This is a stress ball. Today you are going to make your own stress ball to squeeze when you feel stressed. Squeezing the ball can help lower your stress level.

- Give each student three balloons, scissors, and a sandwich bag. Then give the following instructions:

    1. *Cut off the stem of each balloon. This will leave the round part.*

    2. (Optional) *Cut designs into your balloon.*

    3. (Pass the bag of rice/sand around.) *Fill the bottom of your bag with rice (sand). Lay the bag flat. Then fold the bag down until all you see is the rice (sand). Fold the bag in half.*

    4. *Put one balloon over the bag. Do the same with the second balloon, but going in a different direction. When you add the third balloon, make sure your entire bag is covered.*

    The students have created their own stress ball.

- Conclude the session by having each student describe a personally stressful incident while squeezing his/her stress ball. Tell the students they may take their stress balls with them.

SESSION 13
SELF-ESTEEM

Purpose:

To encourage the students to explore things that are meaningful to them

Materials Required:

For the leader:
- ☐ *Group Opening* (page 9)
- ☐ *Group Rules* (page 10)
- ☐ *Energizer 13* (page 33)

For each student:
- ☐ Student's folder
- ☐ *My Personal Shield* (page 268)
- ☐ Pencil
- ☐ Colored markers or pencils

Preparation:

Read the instructions for *Energizer 13*.

Make a copy of *My Personal Shield* for each student.

Session Content:

- Give each student his/her folder.

- Select a student to read the *Group Opening*.

- Pass the *Group Rules* around. Have each student read one rule aloud until all of the rules have been read.

- Present *Energizer 13*.

- Give each student a copy of *My Personal Shield*, a pencil, and colored markers or pencils. Tell the students they are going to make a shield that will represent their personal Coat of Arms.

- Give the following directions, pausing after each step to allow time for the students to complete the task:

    1. *Write a description or draw a picture of your family.*

    2. *Write a description or draw a picture of one thing you would like to change.*

    3. *Write a description or draw a picture of what makes you happiest.*

    4. *Write a description or draw a picture of one of your goals.*

    5. *Write a description or draw a picture of something you like about yourself.*

    6. *Write the name of or draw a picture of someone with whom you would like to get along with better.*

    7. *Write a description or draw a picture of something nice you did for someone recently.*

    8. *Write what you would like others to say about you.*

- Have the students share their personal shields.

- Have the students place their shields in their folders. Collect the folders.

MY PERSONAL SHIELD

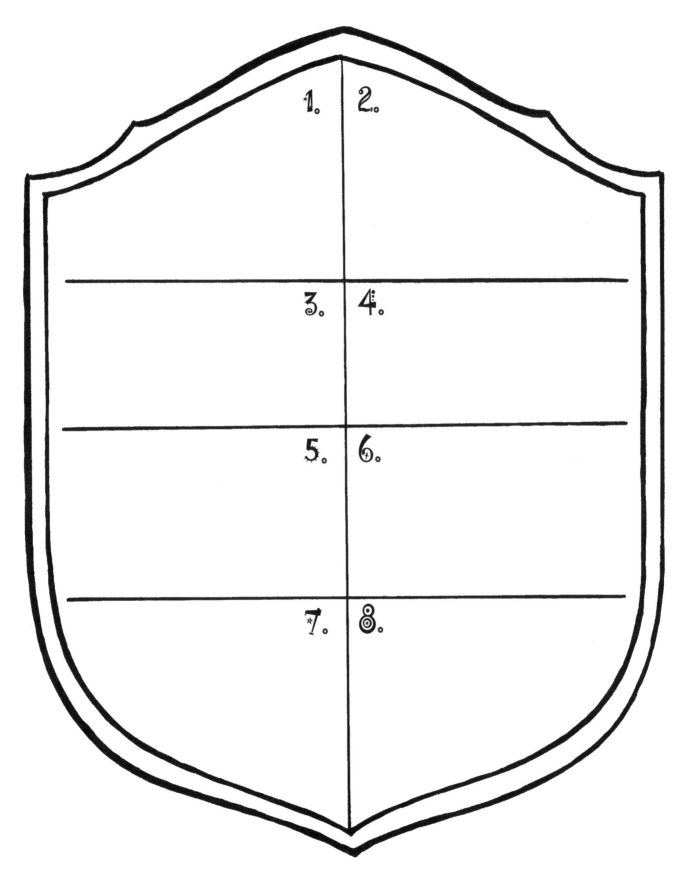

SESSION 14
MORE ON SELF-ESTEEM AND SELF-WORTH BINGO

Purpose:

To help students understand that, depending upon how they react to a situation, they have control over its outcome

Materials Required:

For the leader:
- ☐ *Group Opening* (page 9)
- ☐ *Group Rules* (page 10)
- ☐ *Energizer 11* (page 32)
- ☐ Chalkboard and chalk or dry-erase board and marker
- ☐ *Bingo Numbers* (pages 42-43)
- ☐ Container

For each student:
- ☐ Student's folder
- ☐ *Self-Worth Bingo* (page 271)
- ☐ Markers or pens of two different-color inks

Preparation:

Read the instructions for *Energizer 11*.

Make a copy of *Self-Worth Bingo* for each student.

Make a copy of the *Bingo Numbers*. Cut the numbers apart and place them in the container.

Session Content:

- Give each student his/her folder.

- Select a student to read the *Group Opening*.

- Pass the *Group Rules* around. Have each student read one rule aloud until all of the rules have been read.

- Present *Energizer 11*.

- Tell the students:

    Self-esteem is how you feel about yourself. You have the power to enhance your self-esteem by changing how you feel about yourself.

- Go to the board and write the following formula:

    $$\frac{\begin{array}{l}S \quad \text{(Situation)} \\ + R \quad \text{(Reaction or Response)}\end{array}}{= O \quad \text{(Outcome)}}$$

- Then say:

    How you react or respond to a situation will "equal" or affect the outcome. If you do not like the outcome, you must change how you respond to similar situations to get different outcomes.

    *For example: If the **situation** is homework and your **response** is to not do it, **what is the outcome?*** (Pause for student responses. The students will give various answers such as *failure, possible detention,* and *being grounded*.)

- Have the students use the same example and change the response. For example: If the **situation** is homework and your **response** is to do it, **what is the outcome?** *(Better grades, privileges, etc.)* Emphasize that by changing our reaction or response to a situation, we can often achieve the outcome we want.

- Explain that by replacing negative thoughts about themselves with positive thoughts they can enhance their self-esteem. Give the students the following example:

    If someone says something negative to you, you can say, "Cancel" in your mind. Do not let negative thoughts enter your head. You may also say, "I'm not perfect, but I am the best I can be."

  Have the students give examples of other positive thoughts. Write their ideas on the board.

- Remind the students:

    Do not compare yourselves to others, because doing so often results in low self-esteem. People can always find something about others that they wished they themselves possessed. Be happy with who you are. Chances are, others see something about you that they wish they had.

- Tell the students they are going to play *Self-Worth Bingo*. Give each student a copy of *Self-Worth Bingo* and markers or pens of two different-color inks. Explain how the students should fill in their bingo cards by saying:

    The letters W O R T H are printed at the top of the columns. Below each letter is a number range. Using one color of ink/marker, fill in each circle in each column with one of the numbers within the indicated range. For example, you may choose 3, 5, 8, 12, and 15 to fill in the circles in the column under the letter W.

- Explain how the game is played by saying:

    I will draw one number at a time from this container. As I draw each number, look at your Self-Worth Bingo card to see if you have written that number on your card. If you have that number on your card, raise your hand. I will call on you to complete the sentence written in that space. You may then place an X in the box using the other color of ink/marker. The first person to get five X's in a row should call out Self-Worth Bingo! He or she will win the game.

- Play the game.

- Discuss the statements on the *Self-Worth Bingo* cards. Ask the students which were easy and which were difficult to complete.

- Conclude the session by reminding the students that positive thoughts enhance self-esteem and negative thoughts produce low self-esteem. Think positive!

- Have the students put their bingo cards in their folders. Collect the folders.

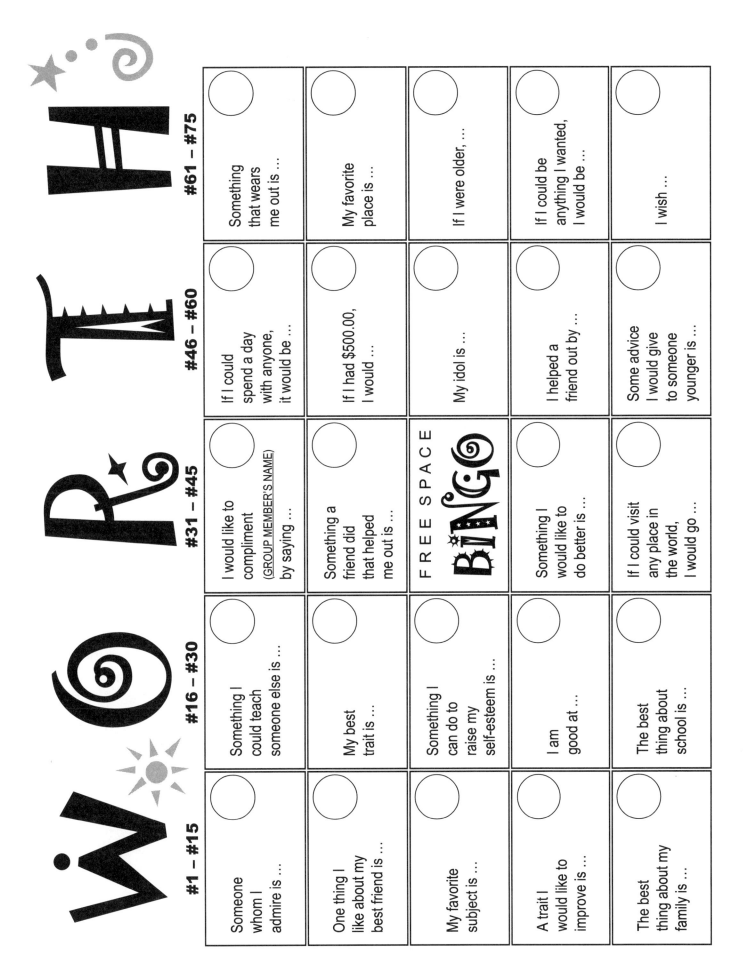

SESSION 15
FINAL GROUP SESSION

Purpose:

To give encouragement to fellow group members and bring closure to the group

Materials Required:

For the leader:
- ☐ *Group Opening* (page 9)
- ☐ *Group Rules* (page 10)
- ☐ Materials for *Energizer 8* (page 31)
- ☐ Materials for *Energizer 10* (page 32)

For each student:
- ☐ Student's folder
- ☐ Index cards
- ☐ Pencil

Preparation:

Read the instructions for *Energizer 8* and *Energizer 10*. Gather the necessary materials.

Session Content:

- Give each student his/her folder and a pencil.

- Select a student to read the *Group Opening*.

- Pass the *Group Rules* around. Have each student read one rule aloud until all of the rules have been read.

- Present *Energizer 8*.

- Give each group member as many index cards as there are students in the group, less one. Feature one group member at a time by having the other students write something nice to him/her. Tell the students to begin with "Dear ____." Make sure each student signs his/her name.

  After each student has been featured, everyone should have an index card from every other student in the group. Tell the students they may keep the cards and read them if they ever start feeling low. They may want to display the cards in their bedroom and read them often.

- Present *Energizer 10*.

- Have the students go through their folders and give you any papers they want shredded. They may keep their folders and any papers they want.

- To conclude the group, have the students participate in the *Jelly Roll Squeeze* activity. Have the students stand side by side with their arms around each other's waists. Beginning on one end, tell the students to start to roll toward the other end. The first person should roll toward the second person, the second person should roll toward the third person, the third toward the fourth, on so on. When everyone is curled in, say, "Squeeze" on the count of three.

- Thank the students for taking part in the group, especially for sharing with others. Remind them to think positively and enhance their own self-esteem.